Everyman's
Book of
British Ballads

Will no one tell me what she sings?
Perhaps the plaintive numbers flow
For old, unhappy, far-off things,
And battles long ago:
Or is it some more humble lay,
Familiar matter of today?
Some natural sorrow, loss, or pain,
That has been, and may be again?

William Wordsworth, 'The Reaper'

The Ballad has been dead, or as good as dead,
for two hundred years.

Sir Arthur Quiller-Couch, *The Oxford Book
of Ballads*, 1910, Introduction

EVERYMAN'S BOOK OF BRITISH BALLADS

edited by Roy Palmer

J M DENT & SONS LTD

London, Melbourne & Toronto

Printed in Great Britain by
Billings Ltd, Guildford, London, Oxford & Worcester for
J M Dent & Sons Ltd
Aldine House, 33 Welbeck Street, London

This book is set in VIP Bembo by
D P Media Ltd, Hitchin, Hertfordshire

British Library Cataloguing in Publication Data

Everyman's book of British ballads.
1. Ballads, English
I. Palmer, Roy
784'.306   M1738
ISBN 0-460-04452-4

CONTENTS

IV AN AWFUL STORY: DEEDS OF DARING

V SENTENCE PASSED: CRIME AND PUNISHMENT

VI TAKE A WARNING FROM ME: CAUTIONARY TALES

VII MY HEART TO YOU: TRUE LOVE AND FALSE

VIII   BOUND TO BE A ROW: LOVE AND MARRIAGE

IX   MARK WELL THE JEST: MERRY TALES

LIST OF ILLUSTRATIONS

P. 21 Woodcut from the original sheet of ballad no. 12, 'The Three Merry Travellers' (Bagford Collection I, 88, published in J. W. Ebsworth (ed.), *The Bagford Ballads*, Hertford, 1878, p. 51).

P. 31 Engraving by Henry Spencer (1785) of 'Robert O'Green, Ballad Singer in Burnley Aetatis 80'. The sheet which Green is holding bears the title: 'Burnley Haymake', which was a satire on a weather-prophet of the day. Reproduced by permission of Fritz Spiegl, *Liverpool Street Songs*, 1966 (4 Windermere Terrace, Liverpool L8 3JB).

P. 44 Woodcut from a broadside entitled 'Rest, Warrior, Rest' (A Collection of Ballads, 1876 e 3). © British Library.

P. 67 Engraving of the late eighteenth century showing an itinerant singer and seller of ballads (*Catchpenny Prints: 163 Popular Engravings from the Eighteenth Century*, Dover Publications, New York, 1970).

P. 71 A print of the late eighteenth century. The entertainment seems to consist of eating, while a piper serenades (*Catchpenny Prints*).

P. 73 Woodcut of a ship in distress, 1800 (*1,000 Quaint Cuts*, Leadenhall Press, n.d.).

P. 83 An embrace. A woodcut by Thomas Bewick, 1753–1828 (H. Thomas, *Bewick's Woodcuts*, 1870).

P. 102 Woodcut from a broadside version of ballad no. 50, 'The Gallant Female Sailor', printed by the famous Catnach, of Seven Dials. By permission of the Broadwood Trust.

P. 127 Woodcut by Thomas Bewick (1753–1828) of a prisoner marking off the days of his confinement on a stick (H. Thomas, *Bewick's Woodcuts*, 1800).

P. 143 A print of the late eighteenth century (*Catchpenny Prints*).

P. 150 A ballad sheet woodcut showing a fiddler confined to the stocks for swearing (Pepys Collection, I, 94). By permission of the Master and Fellows, Magdalene College, Cambridge.

P. 157 Part of the 1656 sheet of 'The Famous Flower of Serving Men', for which see p. 187. (From the Euing Collection of English Broadside Ballads.) By permission of the University of Glasgow.

P. 174 Etching by George Cruickshank from *The Loving Ballad of Lord Bateman*, a joint adaptation by Charles Dickens and W. M. Thackeray of the traditional ballad, 1839.

P. 197 Woodcut from the original sheet of a ballad entitled 'The Patient Husband and the Scoulding Wife' (Roxburghe Collection III, 100, published in W. Chappell and J. W. Ebsworth (eds.), *The Roxburghe Ballads*, Hertford, 1874–91, vol. 7, part 1, p. 74).

P. 218 Woodcut from a ballad sheet of 1675 entitled 'Room for a Jovial Tinker, Old Brass to mend' (cf. our ballad no. 124) (Pepys Collection III, 31). By permission of the Master and Fellows, Magdalene College, Cambridge.

INTRODUCTION

A Handful of Pleasant Delights was the title of the first published collection of ballads, which appeared in 1566. Since then the tide of interest has ebbed and flowed many times, leaving behind an extensive jetsam of ballad books and commentaries. Why, then, yet another anthology?

No other single collection so far has included, with their tunes, ballads of tradition, of the street, of the music hall, and of recent composition – and drawn on material from England, Wales, Scotland and Ireland to boot. The items have at least two things in common: they are, to use James Kinsley's definition, 'narrative songs in which music and poetry are interdependent', something which 'generations of scholars have forgotten' (*The Oxford Book of Ballads*, Oxford, 1969, p. v); and they are all in a traditional idiom, most having survived that form of natural selection which has allowed them to pass into oral currency.

Among narrative ballads I have been looking for fiction rather than fact, story rather than history, largely for the practical reason that I have devoted a number of books to historical narratives, up to and including my *Ballad History of England* (Batsford, 1979). However, I have not been able to resist including ballads about such historical personages as James McPherson (no. 48) and Grace Darling (no. 51), and there are others, too, Sir Patrick Spens, for example (no. 29), who may have really existed. However, the ballads' power lies in dramatic and lyrical narrative. Cleaving to a broadly traditional idiom has enabled me to exclude, for reasons both of space and of personal taste, parlour ballads (except possibly 'The Mistletoe Bough', no. 30), literary imitations, and the productions of the commercial 'popular' and 'pop' song industry.

Thirty-seven items fall within the canon established by Francis J. Child when he gathered his collection of 305 ballads, their known variants, and details of their analogues in other languages (though, for the most part, not their tunes). His monumental work, published in five volumes between 1882 and 1898 under the title of *The English and Scottish Popular Ballads*, includes only one text, 'Judas' (his no. 23), which dates from before 1300, and only a handful from before 1500. Where, then, did the ballads come from – and not only Child's, but some perfectly good examples which he did not accept?

'One of the difficulties about the ballads is that while so much in them seems to be ancient or even primitive, the rhyming ballad verse is comparatively new. Some of the common ballad devices, particularly that of repetition, seem to be as old as anything in humanity, and a large number of ballad subjects are no less widely spread. But the form of verse is not old.' So writes W. P. Ker, 'On the History of the Ballad, 1100–1500' (in *Proceedings of the British Academy*, 1909–10, pp. 179–205). There were plenty of epic narratives and also romances in the Middle Ages, some of which have themes in common with the ballads. It was thought at one time that the ballads were therefore merely fragments of longer narratives, which spread to the lower ranks of society through the efforts of minstrels cast off from aristocratic employment. Yet the ballad, as we shall see, has its own clearly recognizable form, and even if it were solely composed of fragments they would have been recast.

My own conjecture is that the ballad originated in collective work songs. People working together at some rhythmic activity such as rowing, hauling, mowing, frequently sang both to keep time in their work and to lighten its burden. There would be a series of refrains interspersed with solo lines or couplets of narrative. No early examples have survived, which is not surprising; but the centuries-old practice of waulking or fulling cloth to the accompaniment of song existed in the Western Isles of Scotland until within living memory. A length of cloth, having been steeped in urine to take out some of the grease and to shrink it, was pounded, twisted and turned on a board so as further to tighten the fabric. The team of women so engaged would sing, sometimes disjointed texts, but sometimes stories of adventure. Here is part of one song, with the vocables of the refrain and chorus italicized, and the original Gaelic of the narrative lines translated into English:

> *He mandu* if I had
> *He mandu* the sparrow's wing
> *He mandu* the birds' power of flight
> *Hi ri oro* the wild duck's foot
> *He mandu hi ri oro ho ro hu o*
> *He mandu* I would swim
> *He mandu* across the narrows
> *He mandu* the Sound of Islay
> *Hi ri oro* the Sound of Orkney
> *He mandu hi ri oro ho ro hu o*

(Notes to the record, *Music from the Western Isles*, Tangent TNGM 110, 1971; see also the same company's *Waulking Songs from Barra*, TNGM 111, 1972. Both draw on the archives of the School of Scottish Studies.)

The song continues to the effect that the narrator will go to a castle to bring his sweetheart home. It is worth noting that there are mentions of English lacemakers in the nineteenth century singing at their work versions of 'Sir Hugh', 'Death and the Lady' and 'Long Lankin' (*Notes and Queries*, 4th Series, vol. II, pp. 8 and 281), though not necessarily in the manner of the waulking songs.

The alternation of solo narration and collective response, combined with organized activity, reminds one of the singing-dances which follow precisely this pattern still in some parts of Europe, such as Brittany, and also in the Faeroe Islands. In turn, these seem to be descendants of the ancient carols – popular narrative songs accompanied by dancing – which were performed at church wakes and the like. A fragment of one of these has survived from the late thirteenth century in a moralistic Latin poem which describes how a group of dancers at Colbek fell foul of their priests for 'carolling' in the churchyard at Christmas. Despite the presence of his daughter, Ave, in the group, he cursed them. One verse of their song is quoted in the poem, and the translation given here is from an English adaptation of about 1303:

> Equitabat Bovo per silvam frondosam,
> Ducebat sibi Mersuindem formosam;
>   *Quid stamus? cur non imus?*

> By the level wode rode Bevolyne,
> With him he ledde feyre Mersyne;
>   *Why stonde we? why go we noght?*

> (Robert Mannyng, *Handlyng Synne*, in B. Ford (ed.), *The Age of Chaucer*, Harmondsworth, 1959, pp. 262–70; see also G. Paris, *Les Danseurs Maudits*, Paris, 1900.)

The form of both work song and carol, particularly the latter, resembles that of our oldest ballads:

> The miller's daughter, being dressed in red,
> *Hey ho, my Nanny, O;*
> She went for some water to make her bread,
> *Where the swan swims so bonny, O.* (no. 36).

Indeed, A. B. Friedman (*The Ballad Revival*, Chicago, 1961) believes that 'the medieval French dance-song . . . determined the metrical form of the English and Scottish ballads'. He claims that the word, 'ballad', 'entered the language as a result of the naturalization in England of the French *balade* in the late fourteenth century'. The *ballade* was a poetic form of which Villon in the fifteenth century was perhaps the most famous practitioner, with poems such as the *Ballade des Dames du temps jadis*, with its refrain: 'Mais où sont les neiges d'antan?' Friedman goes on to argue that the French *ballade* form, or an approximation to it, was used in England and Scotland in the fifteenth and early sixteenth centuries for politico-religious verse, and when some of this appeared on the early printed sheets, the name, in various forms – ballade, ballet, ballad – became generic. In addition, whereas the earliest examples had not been sung, tunes later began to be indicated. This seems convincing, though as late as about 1500 Dunbar was using the word for what had previously been called a carol: 'And sing ballettis with michty notis clere: / Ladyes to dance full sobirly assayit' (OED).

No doubt the debate will never be concluded to the satisfaction of all parties. Ker has suggested two of the most fruitful ways of avoiding the issue. The first is:

> In spite of Socrates and his logic we may venture to say, in answer to the question 'What is a ballad?' – 'A ballad is *The Milldams of Binnorie* and *Sir Patrick Spens* and *The Douglas Tragedy* and *Lord Randal* and *Child Maurice*, and things of that sort.

The second, and perhaps more useful:

> The 'Ballad' is *form*, and the essence of it is shown in two ways: in the power of taking up new subjects, and treating them according to the laws of the Ballad; and in the lyrical beauty, which is utterly unlike the ballad either of epic poetry or the longer sort of romance.

The form of the ballad depended originally on the traditional singer's technique – he was perhaps also the maker. He would have a story in mind, probably also known to his hearers, limited to a main plot, developing in a few episodes. The structure was very carefully worked out, though its articulation into binary, trinary or annular patterns was able to give great variety and also cohesion. These terms were used by Peter Buchan in his seminal book, *The Ballad and the Folk* (Routledge, 1972). Balance or antithesis can be expressed in a couplet, a stanza, two stanzas, or a whole ballad. Similarly, the progression of three, which is dearly loved in folklore as a whole, can operate within half a stanza ('Ye lee, ye lee, ye liars lood, / Sae lood's I hear ye lee'), in a triad of stanzas, or in a whole ballad with three episodes, sometimes followed by a coda. Finally, 'Framing – the annular device or ring composition, as it is known to the Homerists – is one of the hallmarks of oral poetry, because it is a habit of construction that grows organically out of the restrictive conditions of oral creation' (*op. cit.*, pp. 94–5).

For the early singer, each performance involved a separate recreation of the ballad. Hence a number of set elements used almost as points of rest: stock epithets such as 'the wan water', 'the salt sea', 'lily-white steed'; formulae like 'high hanged you shall be' or 'Woe to

12

you, you wild woman'. Incremental repetition or cumulative iteration is another such device, though it is far from being merely a device, since it can have great emotional charge:

'O, whar'll I get a bonny boy
To hold my helm in hand,
Till I gang to oor topmast tall
To see can I find land?'

'Here ye'll get a bonny boy
To hold your helm in hand,
Till ye gang to oor topmast tall,
But I fear ye'll ne'er find land.'

In many ways, ballad technique is like that of film making. The action often begins *in medias res*, and there is swift cross-cutting from one scene to another, from one person to another, without transition. There are frequent passages of direct speech, without identification of speaker, since this is implicit. The narrative moves swiftly, though this is not to say that all is breakneck action. Just as the camera lingers lovingly at times on details, so, as F. B. Gummere puts it: 'Ballads hold attention to the story by repetition of its main details; they leap or linger, but move straight' (*The Popular Ballad*, Boston, 1907, p. 335). The language is spare and laconic, achieving more by understatement than by rhetoric, though there are reflective moments when the narrator dwells on the implications of grief, death or ingratitude. The view of life is predominantly tragic, and only twenty ballads out of Child's 305 have a happy ending. This might partly be his own choice – and he was very unhappy about bawdy ballads, for example, which seldom have a tragic ending; but it is true to say that the finest of the ballads, 'Lamkin' or 'Little Musgrove' have all the intensity and depth of tragic drama.

To return to the ballad singer: as well as his resources of technique, verbal and structural, he had music. In recent times, most singers have tended to reproduce a set text, but the best have retained the ability to vary the music; indeed, it is scarcely possible to sing all the verses of any ballad without at least some minor change in rhythm, but more than that is needed if the listener's ear, and therefore his mind, are to be fully engaged during a performance. The art singer achieves variety through dynamics – loud, soft, quick, slow, and the gradations between – together with all sorts of changes of colour in the often considerable force of accompanying instruments. The folk singer achieves variety by other means. James Mason's 'Sir Patrick Spens' (no. 29) is a good example. Textually, he had a storehouse of verses, of which he did not necessarily include all in each performance; and some of his individual verses varied from one performance to another. He had two separate tunes, one Ionian and one Hexatonic/Aeolian (not,

13

of course, mixed in one performance). Each was varied from 4/4 time to 5/4 and 6/4. There was considerable melodic variation, as can be seen on page 74. John Reilly in 'The Well below the Valley' (no. 27) also had two tunes, one Ionian (page 68) and one Dorian (given in B. H. Bronson, *The Singing Tradition of the Child Ballads*, Princeton, New Jersey, 1976, p. 83). In Reilly's sixteen-verse Ionian version there is a musical variation for the first line of every single verse, not to speak of many others elsewhere.

Such skill is not confined to the exuberant Scots and Irish. Cecil Sharp was surprised by a blind singer, Henry Larcombe (born 1823) of Haselbury Plucknett in Somerset, whom he met in 1905. The song was 'Robin Hood and the Tanner': 'I remember that . . . he varied the first phrase of the second verse. I asked him to repeat the verse that I might note the variation. He at once gave a third form of the same phrase. I soon learned that it was best not to interrupt him, but to keep him singing the same song over and over again, in some cases for nearly an hour at a time – the patience of these old singers is inexhaustible. In this way I have been able to catch and note down those variations which have occurred two or three times, but, of course, I have missed many of those which have appeared but once.' Sharp makes the comment and gives the variations noted in *Some Conclusions* (4th ed. 1972; first published 1907), and adds that Larcombe was, in his experience, unique. Many singers now available on record – Joseph Taylor of Lincolnshire, Harry Cox of Norfolk, Phil Tanner of the Gower, Robert Cinnamond of Ireland, to mention only a few – have something approaching Larcombe's skill. However, it is fair to add that many singers prefer a relatively plain approach.

Before leaving Mason, Reilly and Larcombe, it is worth commenting on their texts, all of which in various ways demonstrate the tenacity of oral tradition. Mason's full version approximates to a text given in Sir Walter Scott's *Minstrelsy of the Scottish Border* over a century earlier, though he had never seen it in print. Scott himself supplied a fragmentary version of 'The Maid and the Palmer' (Reilly's 'Well') to Charles Kirkpatrick Sharpe in 1825, the only other known version being in Bishop Percy's Folio MS. The ballad was thought defunct – as, indeed, about a hundred of Child's are – until 1969, when Tom Munnelly heard it on Reilly's lips. Since then it has been taken up and recorded by a widely-heard group, Planxty. The ballad has an astonishing capacity for living quietly on for centuries without coming to the attention of scholars; it is passed on by the people themselves because they happen to love it. 'Robin Hood and the Tanner' was published as a black-letter street ballad (see facsimile on page 16) of 37 verses, in 1657. Larcombe had only seven (M. Karpeles, *Cecil Sharp's Collection of English Folk Songs*, 1974, vol. I, pp. 148–9), but they correspond fairly closely with part of the earlier text, down to a phrase

14

'a ground graff', which Sharp queried when noting it. The broadside has: 'another oke graff' (graft?).

There is no hard and fast distinction between traditional ballads on the one hand and broadside ballads on the other. Of the twenty-three broadsides in this collection, at least fifteen have connections with the oral tradition and, conversely, of the 37 Child ballads here over twenty have appeared on broadsides. Indeed, Child's own volumes include many broadside ballads, despite his view that they were 'veritable dunghills in which, only after a great deal of sickening grubbing, one finds a very moderate jewel'. From this and other comments, for example on 'The Auld Wife and the Peat Creel' (no. 115), it is clear that he was deeply disturbed by bawdy songs, yet bawdry is one of the elements in popular culture which constantly recurs. When one reads (August, 1979) that a man in full possession of his senses has suggested that the newly-restored Cerne Abbas Giant needs for reasons of propriety to be partially covered with a loincloth, one can better understand the mentality which drove underground for long periods not only jocular bawdry but deeply serious examinations in ballad form of sexual ethics of every kind.

The oldest broadside ballad extant was printed in about 1530, with the title of 'A Ballad of Luther, the Pope, a Cardinal, and a Husband-man', in the gothic or black-letter type which continued to be used until roughly 1700. From 1650 or so the modern or white-letter type was beginning to come in. It was used throughout the eighteenth and nineteenth centuries, and at the same time ballads tended to grow shorter as the pace of life grew swifter, just as the *tempi* of orchestral music have speeded up in recent years.

It is perhaps true to say that the broadside dwelled more willingly and more extensively on the circumstances of every-day life than the traditional ballads with their 'old, unhappy, far-off things'. Indeed, it has been said that the ballad-singer of the nineteenth century 'with his rough broad-sheet, travelled . . . over the whole surface of man's life, political and social' (*National Review*, 1861). Yet in addition to the events of the day the broadsides also provided entertainment for the people, with their ballads of adventure and escapism, of romance, of earthy humour.

As well as material reprinted from tradition they had many new songs, some of which might pass into oral circulation themselves. The medium was also open to the new writers of the early music hall, such as Ned Corvan (no. 1). The themes and outlook of such writers, who were usually performers themselves, were often on traditional lines, and a music hall audience was by no means passive. A further link between the music hall and tradition is evidenced by the fairly genial parodies of Child ballads which enjoyed a vogue, such as 'Lord Lovel' (no. 96), which, to complete the circle, was also printed as a street

15

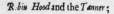

Reference is made to this ballad of 1657 on page 14 (Wood Collection, fol. 9ᵛ – 10ᴿ). ©Bodleian Library.

ballad. Thus a traditional singer at the end of the nineteenth century, such as Henry Burstow (for whom, see my *Everyman's Book of English Country Songs*, 1979, pp. 3 ff.), had ballads of all three kinds in his repertoire.

Such, too, is the case with the professional folk singer of today, with the addition – itself not unknown in tradition – that he also has contemporary songs written by himself or others. Seven examples of such songs are included, and one could have filled the whole volume with them. As it happens, jocular examples are given here, but contemporary ballad makers, like their predecessors, have ranged over 'the whole surface' of life. Just as with literature in general, it seems that there are places and times where exceptional flowerings of balladry occur. The last occasion was in the latter part of the nineteenth century, with the bothy ballads of north-east Scotland. The name comes from the bothies or barrack-like dwellings in which the farm workers lived, and the ballads described in vivid and memorable style work on the land and the conditions of life. The two examples (nos. 73

16

and 110) included here are concerned respectively with a visit to the city and family life, but full justice to the bothy ballads could only be done by a study of John Ord's *Bothy Songs and Ballads* (Paisley, 1930; Edinburgh, 1973). An excellent recent work, unfortunately without music, is D. C. Cameron's *The Ballad and the Plough* (1978), and there is an exceptionally fine record, *Bothy Ballads* (Tangent TNGM 109, 1971), of material from the archives of the School of Scottish Studies.

During the last twenty years or so the narrative ballad has again become acceptable as a mode of creative self-expression. These home-made songs often express the small man's opposition to the impersonal and in some cases sinister monoliths of modern society; sometimes they merely tell a good story. These are not, however, folk songs, but songs in a traditional idiom which may in due course become detached from their makers, enter into independent existence, and eventually gain wide acceptance. Indeed, there are signs that this is already happening with some of the songs of Ewan MacColl, such as 'Shoals of Herring' or 'Forty Foot Trailer'.

The ballads in this volume are exclusively in English. This is not to deny, even by implication, the immense richness and value of the material in the Celtic languages of these islands, but to recognize a practical limitation. Ballads in English from Wales are not at all easy to come by, but there are plenty from Ireland and Scotland. The Irish examples are in fairly straightforward English, but the Scots often have a strong dialectal colouring. The Sassenach will find it worthwhile to persevere with them, for their great strength and power soon come through any linguistic barrier. It is a different matter to attempt to sing them in a pseudo-Scots accent, however. The Englishman would do better to seek a version in his own vernacular where possible, and it is worth remarking that most – though not all – the classic ballads circulated throughout the British Isles. Alternatively, he might even consider remaking a ballad, as Martin Carthy has done with 'Lang Johnny More' (no. 44). No doubt purists will frown on this, but I have a strong feeling that traditional singers have often done the same thing.

For convenience the ballads have been grouped thematically, though none of the categories is by any means water-tight. The first section contains songs of local rivalry, which the folklorists call *blason populaire* (nos. 1 and 2), of preposterous exaggeration (5–8, 13) and of self-indulgent wishful thinking (9, 11, 12). In addition, four (3, 4, 10, 14) show the triumph of superior wit, a quality which even the poorest of the poor can display. Most of the songs are light-hearted, but by no means all: many have undertones of anger, yearning, or even magic.

The supernatural, manifesting itself in various forms, is the thread running through the second section, and it is worth recalling that many ancient beliefs, like old wine in new bottles, subsist even in relatively new ballads. (See, for example, L. C. Wimberly, *Folklore in the English and Scottish Ballads*, Chicago, 1928; reprinted New York, 1965.) The main theme is the two-way pull between the living and the dead (15–21, 27): the living yearn for the dead to return, and occasionally the dead seek to lure the living into the other world. By the same token the ballads are sometimes imbued with almost unbearable human sorrow, and occasionally with malign feelings of hatred and revenge. Shape-changing and magical metamorphoses (22, 23), spells and incantations (24, 25), warning in dreams (26): all these bulk large in the older ballads, though the last listed is one of the most recent. Finally, 'The Cherry Tree Carol' (28) is an example of the many ballads on religious subjects, often, as this one, apocryphal, though none the poorer for that.

Death and suffering occur by no means only in a supernatural context, and the third section deals with these topics. Death by natural forces or accident (29, 30) is hard enough to bear; still harder when the cause is human folly, greed, jealousy, cruelty (31–39). To avoid unrelieved gloom, charity (40) and wisdom (41) have been given an airing. Perhaps the best answer to misfortune and disaster, however, is the courage of men and women. Some of the more ancient ballads show an epic stoicism in the face of adversity, with the hero showing himself superior to whatever overwhelms him simply by his refusal to do other than face it. As Friedman puts it, 'The hero does not ask how man can die better than by facing fearful odds; he faces them, and dies' (*op.cit.*, p. 337). The core of the fourth section (45, 47, 48, 50, 51, 53, 54) consists of ballads with this outlook. In its early forms 'The Draggletail Gipsies' (49) has the same theme, for the lady who has run away with the gipsies declines to return to her lord, even though she faces death. The modern version is much softer, however, and the lady is allowed to make her escape. By no means all heroes were unsuccessful (42, 43), though the cult of the anti-hero (46, 52) has been current much longer than the ideas of Brecht.

While crime of various kinds has already been much in evidence, the fifth section deals specifically with this. The taking of human life, other than in battle, that is, has always aroused horror (55, 56), but various forms of theft are sometimes regarded with greater indulgence. Piracy, whether successful (57) or otherwise (58), is seldom treated unsympathetically. Even if the attitude is favourable, however, tragic consequences often ensue, as with Heather Jock (60), a Scots poacher, Jack Donahue (59), an Irish rebel, and Jack Williams (62), an English thief. Only the peccadillo of the village blacksmith (61) is punished merely by the shame of discovery. Not all ballads of crime are tragic; indeed, many are lighthearted, such as 'The Highwayman Outwitted' (63) – by a 'fair damsel', or those dealing with men suffering as a result of selfish (64), criminal (65) or merely obstreperous women (66). Often there is a strong moralizing element, as when the rake reforms (67) or dies because of venereal disease (68) as a warning to others.

The next section is devoted entirely to cautionary tales, though the moral is sometimes rather amoral. There are warnings against betting (70), drinking (71) and personal vanity (72). The confidence tricks performed by loose women on innocent men, usually sailors or country folk (73–5), seem to have been legion, and the crowning cut in one is that the lady is a ballad seller (76). The country wins at least one victory when a cockney is discomfited (77), but it is a man who puts him to flight in good Corinthian style. It might seem that there is an anti-feminist bias in many ballads, and I suppose that this is true, but the balance is redressed by frequent warnings of men's perfidy, such as 'Rosemary Lane' (78), with its practical advice: 'Now all you young lasses/Take a warning by me;/Never trust a young sailor/Whoe'er he may be', with the last couplet sometimes being even more to the point: 'Never trust a young sailor/An inch above your knee'. In 'The Fair Maid of Islington' (79) a rich man tries to avoid paying after enjoying the favours of a poor woman, but she turns the tables on him by using her sharp wit in the manner beloved throughout folk litera-ture. Some of the tales, while overtly cautionary (80, 81) concentrate far more on enjoying the plight of the protagonists than promoting a reform of morals. There are some genuine warnings (82), however, and an occasional *memento mori* (83) is no doubt salutary.

Ballads of love, courtship and marriage make up the majority of those current in the British Isles. The seventh section deals with true and false love, beginning with the joys and sorrows of courtship (84, 85). Unacceptable suitors must sometimes be strongly resisted (86, 87, 91); conversely, a desired partner must sometimes be fought for (88, 90, 92, 93). The pangs of lost love are treated very movingly (95–7). The trials of courtship are sometimes followed by the tribula-tions of marriage, which are covered in the next section. Even if the right spouse is carefully selected (98–100), problems can still arise (104–9), which sometimes result in married people seeking relation-ships outside wedlock (101–3). However, some do arrive at happi-ness, or at least moderate contentment (110, 111).

The last section consists of merry tales, most of which, as the adjective used to imply, are of a sexual nature. Various forms of discomfiture, particularly when they involve nudity (112), the private parts (113) or sexual imbroglio (114), are staple material for comedy. More positively, most of the ballads here tell of sexual triumph, though a man's satisfaction can be a woman's sorrow or vexation (116). Often both parties are well satisfied, if necessary *contra mundum* (115–18, 121, 122). Good fortune in love as well as sexual athleticism have an appeal especially when tempered with wit (123, 124), or when

19

a working man enjoys the favours of his employer's wife (119, 120). Finally, unabashed sensuality never seems to come amiss (126).

This, then, is a collection of stories, and it must stand or fall primarily on whether the narratives can hold the attention of a listener (or reader) of today. The worth of any story derives partly from its subject matter, but partly also from its telling. The same joke, the same anecdote, the same tale, can succeed or fail in the mouths of different narrators, depending on their grasp or otherwise of the art of story-telling. Prose narratives do not concern us here, but the art of the ballad maker does, since he is the narrator, through the mouth of a singer.

The word art is not misplaced, because these ballads have a form, a style, an aesthetic system. They – or most of them, since some are new – are part of the heritage of popular culture, which was once common to all. Even as recently as the nineteenth century many well-to-do people knew the rhymes, tales and songs of ordinary humanity through their servants and nurses. Present society is fragmented, and a common culture is lacking. Even the words of the Authorized Version of the Bible, which rang through the centuries wherever English was spoken, have been trivialized in 'easy' or 'everyday' new translations.

These ballads deserve another hearing. They should not be parroted, but re-created musically, according to traditional practice. We should look to them for their intrinsic merits, but also for what they can offer us today. We should use them as models for the making of new songs.

I
Who Hung the Monkey?
Tall Stories

1   Who Hung the Monkey?

The story goes that during the wars with France (1793–1815) an unfortunate monkey, the mascot on a man o' war, fell overboard and was washed ashore at Hartlepool. His inability to communicate in English, coupled with his outlandish appearance, led the local people to believe that he was a French spy, and he was summarily hanged on the Town Moor. The song, to the tune of 'The Tinker's Wedding', was written by Ned Corvan (1830–65) of Tyneside, and performed 'with immense applause' at the Dock Hotel Music Hall in Hartlepool. Since Corvan's day things seem to have changed, and the cry from the opposing terraces of 'Who hung the monkey?' is calculated, I am reliably informed, to provoke immediate rage and violent retaliation from the supporters of Hartlepool United.

In for-mer times when war and strife From o'er the Channel threat-ened life, When all was ready for the knife To watch the French-men, fun-ky, O! The fish-er-men with cou-rage high Seized what they thought a real French spy. 'Kill him,' says yan, 'up with him to die.' They did, and they hung the mon-key, O! Dir-rim day, do a day, dir-rim do a dad-dy, O! Dir-rim day, do a day. They did, and they hung the mon-key, O!

2 They tried every move to make him speak,
They tortured Pug till he loud did squeak.
'That's French,' said one; says another, 'It's Greek.'
The fishermen then got drunky, O!
'He has hair all over,' the wives did cry;
'Oh, what-un a woman with him would lie.'
With fish guts then they bunged up his eye,
Before they hung the monkey, O!

3 Now some the monkey did bewail,
For although dumb he had a tale (tail);
He'd sooner p'raps have gone to jail,
For Pug was turning funky, O!
The monkey made some curious mugs
When they shaved his head and clipped his lugs,
Saying, 'This is t'way to serve humbugs,'
Before they hung the monkey, O!

4 'Hammer his ribs, the thundering thief;
Pummel his peyte weel, man, wi' your neef;
He's landed here for nought but grief,
He's old Napoleon's uncky, O!'
To poor Pug thus all hands behaved:
'Cut off his jimmy,' some fools raved;
Another cries out, 'He's never been shaved,'
Before they hung the monkey, O!

22

5 Then they put him on a grid-iron hot:
   The monkey then quite lively got;
   He grinned his teeth at all the lot
   And rolled his eyes quite spunky, O!
   Then a fisherman up to poor pug goes,
   Saying, 'Let's hang him at once to end his woes';
   The monkey flew at him and bit off his nose,
   Then they off to the Moor with the monkey, O!

6 But let us hope that on the sea
   We'll still maintain our sovereignty;
   May France and England long agree,
   And never at each other get funky, O!
   As regards poor Pug, I've had my say,
   And former times have passed away;
   Still you may hear to this very day
   Boys crying, 'Who hung the monkey, O?'

yan: one.   *neef*: knife.

2   The Congleton Bear

You young men of Che-shire I'd have you to be-ware Of the
peo-ple and the plea-sures of Con-gle-ton Fair; In Con-gle-ton
Bear Town where mo-ney for to save, The Bi-ble it-self for a
new bear they gave. Con-gle-ton rare, Con-gle-ton
rare, They sold the church Bi-ble to buy a new bear.

2 A new Bible was wanted, the old book was done;
  All the people agreed to subscribe to the sum.
  At length they collected the money required,
  To the joy of the parson, the clerk and the choir.

3 But the old bear decided it was time for a change,
  And the week before the wakes was due he died of the mange.
  A new bear was needed, nobody could deny;
  The thought of the wakes was unbearably nigh.

4 When somebody whispered: 'The old book will do,
  It's lasted us now for a good year or two;
  With the parson's collection we'll buy a new bear.'
  All the people agreed this decision was fair.

5 The parson preached daily of Congleton's shame,
  The clerk wrote it down, the choir sang this refrain:
  In Congleton Bear Town where money for to save,
  The Bible itself for a new bear they gave.

Rivalry between neighbouring communities, perhaps with its roots in distant disputes about territory and boundaries, engendered mutual contempt, suspicion, mistrust, hatred, ridicule. These feelings were expressed in actions and in words, the latter in a great fund of stories, rhymes and songs. The people of Congleton in Cheshire were never allowed to live down the alleged sale of their town Bible in 1601 to raise money for a new bear. Peter Coe has cast the story into song, with the charitable gloss that money collected for a new Bible was used, rather than money from selling one.

3   The Doctor Outwitted by the Black

When medicine enjoyed a boom in the late eighteenth and early nineteenth centuries the number of bodies available for dissection fell far below the demand. Only the bodies of criminals and paupers might legally be used (that is, until the Anatomy Act of 1832), so the supply was increased illegally, either by cold-blooded killing, as in the case of the infamous Burke, or by robbing fresh graves. The illicit traffic in bodies aroused understandable indignation against the body snatchers, and also against doctors. This song seems to have originated in Ireland, though it was found in oral circulation in North America under such titles as 'The Black Cook' and 'The Black Devil' until as recently as the 1950s.

I'll tell you a trick that was played t'o-ther eve-ning On an e-mi-nent sur-geon that dwells in this town; By a sai-lor so bold he was out-wit-ted nice-ly, And fif-ty bright shillings he had to pay down. These jol-ly jack tars — and mess-mates being groggy, Their cash it being spent and their credit far run, Through West-mor-land Street for the quay they did ram-ble, Being bent to pro-cure ei-ther money or fun.

2 The cook of the vessel being one of the party –
  A smart lad he was, though his colour was black;
  For wit and contrivance he never was wanting,
  For he found a way to raise cash in a crack –
  Says he to his messmates: 'I hear people talking
  That a corpse can be sold very readily here,
  So take me alive, roll me up in my hammock,
  And fifty bright shillings to you I will pay.'

3 Then they took the hint and the sailors next morning
  Went into a shop where a doctor did dwell;
  In the ear of the doctor they slowly did whisper,
  Saying, 'Sir, we have got a fine corpse for to sell.'
  'A corpse,' says the doctor, like one in amazement,
  'Bring it to me. Where have you got it, I pray?
  Come bring it safe here and I'll buy it quite ready,
  And fifty bright shillings to you I will give.'

4 The sailors agreed and accepted the offer;
  Away to the ship then they did repair.
  I pray you will listen and pay good attention:
  You'll hear very soon what they went to do there.
  They rolled the black up with his hammock about him –
  He was a fine fellow both sturdy and strong –
  And stuck in his waistcoat by way of protection
  A knife with a blade about half a yard long.

5 Twelve o'clock being come and the streets being silent,
  The sailors set off with the black on their back,
  And up to the doctor they slowly did venture
  And in the back room they concealed the poor black.
  The doctor he paid the bold seamen their money,
  And they said their cook he had died on the sea:
  'So sooner than have his dead body to bury
  We sold him to you and he's out of the way.'

6 So the sailors departed and went to a tavern
  Where they had agreed the black for to meet.
  I pray you will listen and pay good attention:
  The best of my story I have to tell yet.
  The doctor ran up for a knife to dissect him,
  And quickly came down with his tools in his hand
  Into the room where he left the corpse lying,
  But the black with his cutlass there ready did stand.

7 When into the room the doctor did enter
  He thought the poor cook was a very rich prize,
  But with voice loud as thunder the black did approach him,
  Saying, 'Damn your eyes, doctor, I'll dissect you alive.'
  The doctor he ran like one was distracted,
  And into the room to his wife tumbled in,
  Saying, 'Dear, oh dear, now where will you hide me?
  For surely the devil is in the back room.'

8 His wife she ran to the door in a hurry
  And bolted it fast that he could not come in.
  She said, 'My dear husband, give over dissecting,
  For fear the black devil might come back again.'

The doctor was glad to retreat in a hurry,
And for his late bargain was soon to repent,
While the black went to where his messmates were drinking,
And the rest of the night they merrily spent.

4   The Private Still

*The exercise of superior wit is a perennial theme of folktale and ballad. Here
the unpopular gauger (exciseman) is outwitted.*

A gau - ger once in Dub - lin town, the time that I was
there, He fan - cied that a pri - vate still was be - ing wrought some-
- where; He met me out one mor - ning, p'raps he fan - cied that I
knew. 'Oh, ne - ver mind,' said he, 'Pat, how do you
do?' With my fol - ol - dtha - di - do, fol - ol - dtha - dee.

2 'I'm pretty well, your honour, but allow me for to say,
I don't know you at all.' Said he, 'Perhaps you may.
I'm going to find a something out, assist me if you will,
Here's fifty pounds if you can tell where there's a private still.'

3 'Give me the fifty pounds,' said I, 'i' faith I surely can;
I'll keep my word, you may depend, as I'm an Irishman.'
The fifty pounds he then paid down, I pocketed the fee;
'Now button up your coat,' said I, 'and come along with me.'

4 As soon as we are on the car, said he, 'Now tell me, Pat,
Where is that blessed private still? Don't take me for a flat.'
'A flat, your honour? No,' said I, 'but hear me if you will,
And I at once will let you know where there's a private still.

27

5 'In half a minute now,' said I, 'the barrack's close at hand,
   And if you look right through the gate you'll see and hear the
       band;
   And when the band's done playing you will see the soldiers
       drill.'
   'Oh, never mind the soldiers, Pat, but where's the private
       still?'

6 'In just a second now,' said I, 'I'll point him out to you.
   See! There he is, that fat old chap, standing between them
       two.'
   'What is that you say?' said he. Said I, 'My brother Bill:
   They won't make him a corporal, so he's a private still.'

7 The gauger swore and tore his hair to get his money back,
   But I jumped on the car myself and bolted in a crack.
   And as he walks along the road, though sore against his will,
   The people shout: 'Exciseman, have you got the private still?'

Private still: for distilling illicit poteen. *car*: tram. *flat*: fool (opposite of sharp).

5   Wha's Fu'?

*The good-humoured topsy-turvydom of this song has been current for some
four centuries. 'Martyn said to his man, whoe is the foole now' was registered
as a ballad in 1588, though the earliest surviving copy of the tune and text is in
Ravenscroft's* Deuteromelia *of 1609. It has been suggested that the English
song may derive from an even older Scots original, since 'Who's the fool now?'
may be an Anglicization of 'Wha's fu' the noo?' ('Who's drunk now?').*

I saw a midge u-pon a stee-ple, Wha's fu', wha's fu'? I
saw a midge u-pon a stee-ple, Wha's fu' the noo? __ I saw a midge u-pon a stee-ple
Pee-in' down on a' the people. You're all blind drunk, my boys, And I'm jol-ly fu'. __

2 I saw a snail chase a whale
  Around aboot the purridge pail.

3 I saw an eel chase the deil
  Aroond aboot the tattie field.

4 I saw a loose chase a moose
  Aroond the riggin' o' a hoose.

5 I saw a soo showin' silk
  Aroon aboot a bowl of milk.

6 I saw a sheep shearin' corn
  With a hook aboot its horns.

7 I saw a duck shoe a horse
  A' with a hammer in its arse.

8 I saw the man in the moon
  Drivin' tackets in his shoon.

9 I saw the sun shinin' bricht
  In the middle o' the nicht.

loose, moose, hoose: louse, mouse, house.   *tackets*: tacks.

6   **Sandy Dawe**

There is a strange fascination in this chain of surreal events. The rhyme was first printed in 1784, but remained current until recent years (see I. and P. Opie, The Oxford Dictionary of Nursery Rhymes, 1977, no. 322). In North Yorkshire, Richard Blakeborough remembered recitations by the kitchen fire, 'the maid sitting by the table with her hand near the lighted candle; towards the last few lines her voice would drop, until, on repeating the last line, it almost became a whisper. With ears strained, and eyes nearly out of our heads, we awaited the dramatic dénouement, which most of us well knew; but in those days the excitement never waned, always the same intensity of feeling was duly worked up, as she repeated in a hoarse whisper, 'dead, dead, dead indeed', extinguishing the light, as she uttered the last syllable with a fearful shriek, whilst we all yelled in one mighty chorus' (Wit, Character, Folklore and Customs of the North Riding of Yorkshire, 1898, p. 269). Our version is from Ayrshire, with some verses added from Blakeborough.

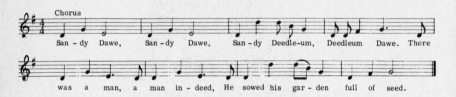

San - dy Dawe, San - dy Dawe, San - dy Deedle-um, Deedleum Dawe. There was a man, a man in - deed, He sowed his gar - den full of seed.

2 When the seed began to grow,
'Twas like a garden full of snow.

3 When the snow began to melt,
'Twas like a ship without a belt.

4 When the ship began to sail,
['Twas like a bird without a sail.

5 When the bird began to fly,
'Twas like an eagle in the sky.

6 When the sky began to roar,
'Twas like a lion at my door.

7 When my door began to crack,
'Twas like a penknife at my back.

8 And when my back began to bleed,
I was dead, dead, dead indeed].

Robert Green, Ballad singer in Burnley Ætatis 80.

7   Paddy and the Whale

The highly improbable, not to say impossible, notion of a man being swallowed whole by a whale, then regurgitated alive, has been a source of fascination ever since Jonah. The celebrated Baron Munchausen, whose adventures were first published in English in 1785, made his escape by so annoying the whale with his dancing of hornpipes in its belly that the animal was only too glad to get rid of him. Paddy's encounter is one of a whole series in which the innocent abroad meets for the first time such technological marvels as balloons, railways, canals and sailing ships. The whale was just as big a marvel. At first, disaster impends, but everything turns out for the best.

2 Now Paddy had never been whaling before,
   And his heart gave a jump when he heard a loud roar.
   'Twas a lookout who cried when the whale he did spy;
   'We'll be all eaten up,' says Pat, 'by and by.'

3 Well, Paddy ran forward, got hold of the mast,
   And he wrapped his arms round and held it so fast;
   And the ship gave a lurch, boys, and then he did slip,
   Straight down to the whale's belly now Paddy did slip.

4 He was down in that whale for six months and five days.
   When one day by chance in the whale's mouth he strayed;
   And the whale gave a cough, boys, and then it did blow:
   Straight out on dry land now poor Paddy did go.

5 And now that he's safely back home on the shore
   He swears that he'll never go whaling no more;
   And the next time he's wishful for Greenland to see
   'Twill be when the railways run over the sea.

8   The Christmas Hare

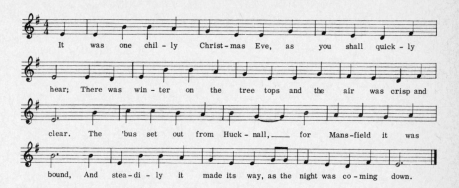

It was one chil-ly Christ-mas Eve, as you shall quick-ly hear; There was win-ter on the tree tops and the air was crisp and clear. The 'bus set out from Huck-nall, ___ for Mans-field it was bound, And stea-di-ly it made its way, as the night was co-ming down.

2 It was down by Newstead woodside as we were passing there,
From out behind a thicket ran a bonny black hare;
Down the road she started and she set a cracking pace,
And the driver shouted 'Tally ho' and after her gave chase.

3 Then he revved up his engine, crying, 'hark, hark away';
The spirit of the chase it fairly carried him away;
And as we swung along the road to the music of his horn
We thought that we would never live to see the Christmas
    morn.

4 Arms and legs were flying as we lurched around the bends;
Wives clung on to husbands and friends clung on to friends.
The conductor rang his bell like mad but the driver took no
    heed,
Or else he took it for encouragement, for he quickened up his
    speed.

5 And in Newstead and in Annesley they stand and stare,
    aghast,
For to hear a 'bus's engine and a hare comes running past.
Imagine their amazement as they wondered what was up
When the 'bus went flying past and left them standing at the
    stop.

6 Now she never looked behind her and she ran so straight and
    true,
But the chase was nearly over when East Kirby came in view;

For, coming past the *Badger Box* and up to Mutton Hill,
The hare began to tire – it was time to make the kill.

7 Then all at once the 'bus stopped dead and we landed on the
    floor
And, looking out the window, hare and huntsman saw.
He held her by the legs, saying, 'Isn't she a winner?
I've a wife and seven kids at home, and here's a Christmas
    dinner.'

Badger Box: public house at Annesley.

To the acute discomfiture of his passengers, a driver uses his 'bus to pursue along the road a hare, rabbit or fox. This story, in various forms, still circulates in parts of Derbyshire and Nottinghamshire. One version was put into song by Roger Watson, whose grandmother heard in the 1920s the tale of a frantic drive one Christmas Eve along the road between Hucknall and Mansfield. The tune is a light-hearted variant on 'God Rest Ye Merry, Gentlemen'.

9   Lancashire Dick

For a poor weaver in the hungry 1840s, Lancashire must have been a grim place. A fantasy like this must have helped to make life a little more bearable. It is remarkably like a Chaplin film: jaunty, full of longing, escapist, yet with a firm grasp of social reality.

It is now for a new song, gentlemen all, Perhaps you've not heard of my sad downfall. I had three pair of looms, they're taken for rent By three bumbailiffs from Manchester sent. O poor Dicky, I think it's a pity, I've nothing to work on, pray what shall I do?

2 I've five little children, my wife she is lame,
  My neighbours all round well know the same.
  Thin water gruel for my children I make,
  For no flour have I in loaves for to bake.

3 I to Manchester market one Saturday went,
  For to buy a few things it was my intent.
  I had seven shillings tied up in a rag:
  Stole out of my pocket – then I got the bag.

4 Potatoes I wanted, and full half a score;
  I went to a man I had bought on afore.
  I begged he would trust, but he rudely said 'Nay:
  We can have such good customers every day.'

5 You may think poor Dicky was here at a stand,
  Not knowing what plan he should now take in hand.
  I went to a shop then for two pounds of meal;
  Says the shopman, 'Your cash, sir, or else we can't deal.'

6 You may very well think my case it was bad,
  No money at all and no trust to be had;
  But now I am better, I had need not to care:
  My uncle has left me five thousand a year.

New Chorus

  O fine Dicky, I think it is pretty,
  Plenty of money and nothing to do.

7 I strut through the streets and look very big,
  With a new pair of boots and powdered wig.
  I've a new gig a-making, to London I'll go,
  And will use endeavours to bring markets low.

8 If a Parliament man I should happen to be,
  A friend to the poor I surely will be;
  For peace and good trade I'll speak like a man,
  And take off the Corn Bill as soon as I can.

9 Of beef and pudding I'll have my fill;
   In my two-arm chair then sing I will.
   Success to my uncle for being so brave,
   And Lancashire Dick no more porridge shall have.

three pair of looms: this means three looms (cf. three pairs of trousers).
bumbailiffs: sheriff's officers, bailiffs.
Manchester market: at Shudehill.
got the bag: got the sack; was rejected.
Corn Bill: the Corn Laws were repealed in 1846.

10   Dixie's Dog

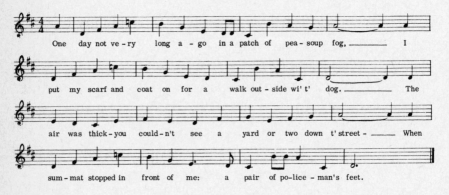

One day not ve-ry long a-go in a patch of pea-soup fog, _____ I
put my scarf and coat on for a walk out-side wi' t' dog. _____ The
air was thick-you could-n't see a yard or two down t' street - _____ When
sum-mat stopped in front of me: a pair of po-lice-man's feet.

2 There grew from them some trousers, they were dyed in
      navy-blue,
   A helmet, a coat, a pair of hands, with a notebook in them,
      too.
   I pretends I hasn't seen 'im, like, there being so much fog,
   Then a thund'rous voice booms out, 'Now where's your
      licence for your dog?'

3 Well, times were bad and jobs were scarce, and I'd had to go
      on t' dole,
   And all the brass I'd scraped together I'd spent on food and
      coal.
   He knew I had no licence, he were kicking up a fuss,
   He says, 'Bring it in tomorrow, or you'll be having tea with
      us.'

36

4 So all next day I sat at home and studied chimney flue,
  Wondering if he'd come around, and thinking what to do.
  Then I heard a noise at top o' t' road, it sounded like flat feet,
  And I knew it were that copper as he trundled down the street.

5 So I hid myself behind the door as he began to knock:
  He'd no idea I were so near – I could even smell his socks.
  When he got tired he went away and I brewed me a cup o' tea,
  And I thowt whatever happened, last laugh'd be on me.

6 So next day two burly rozzers come a-swaggering in the
    place,
  And I had my licence ready and grin all o'er my face.
  He says, 'Eh up, you were stony broke when I met you in the
    fog.
  How can you afford a licence?' I said, 'I've sold my bloody
    dog.'

'The story was told to me by a real old cock in the Wheatsheaf *in Bolton. He said it happened to him in the 1930s. I simply wrote it into verse and added a tune.' Thus Bernard Wrigley, himself a native of Bolton, whose song can be heard on the record,* The Phenomenal B. Wrigley *(Topic 12TS211, 1971).*

11   The Pear Tree

Viewed in a certain light, the narrator here is a voyeur and a thief. However, the manner in which a tale is told is all-important, and this song is light-hearted and good-humoured. It has seldom been seen in print, and this version comes from the repertoire of Frank Hinchliffe of South Yorkshire.

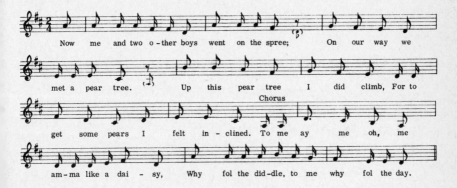

Now me and two o-ther boys went on the spree; On our way we
met a pear tree. Up this pear tree I did climb, For to
get some pears I felt in-clined. To me ay me oh, me
am-ma like a dai - sy, Why fol the did-dle, to me why fol the day.

2 When up this pear tree I'd got landed
(The other two lads from me they'd squandered),
Were not the pears that pleasèd me,
But a man and a woman came under the tree.

3 Now with sweet kisses he embraced her,
Swore for many a mile he'd chased her;
Pulled off his coat to save her gown,
And he gently sits this fair maid down.

4 Now I shook this pear tree just like thunder;
The man and the woman ran away in wonder.
Were not the pears that pleasèd me,
But a damn' good coat left under the tree.

5 Now off to town I ran like fire,
The owner of the coat being my desire;
The owner of the coat were nivver found out,
So I got a damn' good coat for nowt.

6 Come all ye lads wherever you may be,
Nivver go a-courtin under a pear tree;
Nivver pull your coats off to save their gowns,
For the pears they will come tumbling down.

squandered: sc. wandered.   *nowt*: rhymes here with 'boat'.

12   The Three Merry Travellers

Stories abound of the remission of debts in exchange for sexual favours. Modern examples feature the milkman or door-to-door salesman, with housewives as debtors. Here, very unusually, it is three men who pay their bills in full 'without ever a stiver [smallest coin] of money'. 'The Jovial Companions, Or, The Three Merry Travellers' was first published in about 1685, though its 'Excellent North-Country Tune' was – and indeed the ballad itself might have been – in existence at least a century earlier.

There was three Tra-vel-lers, Tra-vel-lers three, with a
hye down, ho down, Lank-tre down der-ry, And they wou'd go Tra-vel the
North Coun-try, without e-ver a sti-ver of Mo-ny.

2 They Travelled *East*, and they travelled *West*,
Where ever they came still they drank of the best.

3 At length by good Fortune they came to an Inn,
And they were as Merry as e'er they had been.

4 A Jolly young Widow did smiling appear,
Who drest them a Banquet of delicate cheer.

5 Both Chickens and sparrow grass she did provide,
You'r Welcome kind Gentlemen, welcome (she cry'd).

6 They called for liquor, both Beer, Ale, and Wine,
And every thing that was curious and fine.

7 They drank to their Hostess a merry full bowl,
She pledg'd them in love like a generous Soul.

8 The Hostess, her Maid, and [her] Cousin all three,
They Kist and was merry, as merry cou'd be.

9 Full Bottles and Glasses replenisht the Board;
No Liquors was wanting the house cou'd afford.

10 When they had been Merry a good part of the day,
They called their Hostess to know what's to pay.

11 There's Thirty good shilling and Six pence, (she cry'd)
They told her that she should be soon satisfy'd.

12 The Handsomest Man of the three up he got,
He laid her on her Back, and paid her the shot.

13 The middlemost Man to her Cousin he went,
   She being Handsome, he gave her content.

14 The last Man of all he took up with the Maid,
   And thus the whole shot it was Lovingly paid.

15 The Hostess, the Cousin, and Servant, we find,
   Made Courchies, and thankt them for being so kind.

16 The Hostess said, welcome kind Gentlemen, all,
   If you chance to come this way be pleased to Call.

17 Then taking their Leaves they went merrily out,
   And they'r gone for to Travel the Nation about.

sparrow grass: asparagus(?)   *Courchies*: curtsies.

13   O'Reilly and Big MacNeil

The day I met O' Reil-ly _____ it was thir-ty-two be-low, _____ The sparks were fly-ing off his pick, he was up to his neck in snow; _____ His foot-steps shook the base-ment slabs, I saw the sky turn black, _____ And O' Reil-ly cried, 'I'm your gan-ger, noo, so dig un-til you crack.' _____ For he was big-ger than a dum-per truck, he'd legs like con-crete piles, _____ His face was like a ton o' bricks and his teeth were six-inch files; _____ His eyes they shone like dan-ger lamps, his fists were tough as steel, _____ But a man as wee as that was ne-ver a match for big Mac-Neill. _____

2 When the tea came round at dinner time he grabbed a gallon
      tin.
   I said, 'Ye'd better put that doon if ye would save your skin.
   You may be cried O'Reilly but I will to ye reveal,
   The can o' tea you've in your hand belangs to big MacNeil.'

3 Well, he laughed at me and he carried on as if I hadnae spoke,
   Says he to me, 'A Dublin man can always take a joke';
   But when he grabbed a shovel, wee Jimmy gave a squeal:
   'Ye'd better leave that spoon alone, it belongs to big
      MacNeil.'

4 Everything the ganger touched we told him to leave alone,
   Or else MacNeil would grind him up, make plaster of his
      bones,
   Until at length he lost the rag and said he'd make a meal
   Of any man in this squad, especially big MacNeil.

5 We said MacNeil was ill but we told him where to go;
   The lads all downed their tools and went alang to watch the
      show.
   As they gaed up Jamaica Street wee Jimmy danced a reel
   To see him hammering at the door of our hero, big MacNeil.

6 And when he got inside there was a monster on the bed,
   With a body as big as a stanchion base and a barrel-size o' head;
   He thumped him, he jumped him, he kicked his head wi' zeal,
   When the missus cried, 'Don't hurt my wean or else I'll tell
      MacNeil'.

cried: called.   *wean:* baby.

*The Big Hewer of mining folklore is one of the legendary supermen of modern
industry. Another, Tiny Newman of Oxford, was a real man who lived in the
1930s and could fit motor tyres with his bare hands. Big MacNeil, in this song
by Donneil Kennedy, is a Glaswegian navvy from the same mould.*

14   The Old Woman and Her Pig

This story is so widespread that it has a number (2030) in the international index of tale-types. The fascination lies in the accumulation of seemingly insoluble problems. Eventually, a key is found and there is a chain reaction which brings a most satisfying resolution. More than a suspicion remains that a spell has been unlocked by the appropriate charm, and this should perhaps be regarded less as a tall story than a piece of good magic.

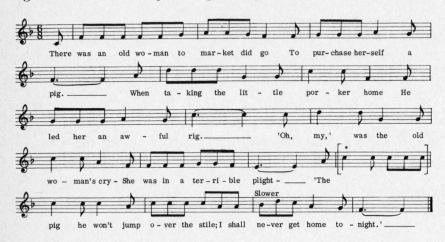

There was an old wo-man to mar-ket did go To pur-chase her-self a pig. ____ When ta-king the lit - tle por - ker home He led her an aw - ful rig. ____ 'Oh, my,' was the old wo - man's cry - She was in a ter-ri - ble plight - ____ 'The pig he won't jump o - ver the stile; I shall ne-ver get home to - night.' ____

Slower

* Repeat this bar ad lib. in succeeding verses.

2 The old woman saw a dog passing by
  When she'd waited a little while.
  'Good doggie,' said she, 'will you bite the pig
  And make him jump over the stile?
  Oh my', was the old woman's cry –
  She was in a terrible plight –
  'Dog won't bite pig; pig won't jump stile;
  I shall never get home tonight.'

3 The old woman saw a stick lying by
  When she'd waited a little while.
  'Good stick,' said she, 'will you beat the dog,
  For the dog to bite the pig to jump the stile?
  Oh my,' was the old woman's cry –
  She was in a terrible plight –
  'Stick won't beat dog, dog won't bite pig, pig won't jump
        style;
  I shall never get home tonight.'

4 The old woman saw a blazing fire
  When she'd waited another little while.
  'Good fire,' said she, 'will you please burn the stick,
  The stick to beat the dog, the dog to bite the pig, the pig to
        jump the stile?
  . . . Fire won't burn stick; stick won't beat dog . . .' *etc.*

5 The old woman saw a pool of water
  When she'd waited a little while.
  'Good water,' said she, 'will you squinch the fire,
  The fire to burn the stick, the stick to beat the dog . . . ? *etc.*
  . . . Water won't squinch fire; fire won't burn stick; . . .' *etc.*

6 So the old woman saw an ox passing by
  And he came near the stile.
  'Good ox,' said she, 'will you drink the water, the water to
        squinch the fire . . . ? *etc.*
  . . . Ox won't drink water; water won't squinch fire . . .' *etc.*

7 [So the old woman saw a butcher passing by
  As he came near the stile.]
  The butcher began to kill the ox, the ox to drink the water;
  The water began to squinch the fire, the fire to burn the stick;
  The stick began to beat the dog,
  (*Spoken*) Dog to bite the pig, the pig to jump the stile.
  'Oh my,' was the old woman's cry,
  'I'm not in such a terrible plight.'
  The little pig he jumped over the stile,
  And the old woman got home that night.

II
Cold Blows the Wind:
the Supernatural

15   The Wife of Usher's Well

1. There was a la — dy and la — dy — like, And chil — dren she had three. She sent them a — way to a north — ron school —— To learn their gram — mar — ye.

2 They hadn't been gone but a very short time,
Scarcely six months and three days,
When death strayed abroad in all that land
And swept her three babes away.

3 'Why mourn ye for your gowd, your gowd,
And for your white money?'
'I do mourn for my three bonnie sons
That death has ta'en fae me.

4 'I'll hie me doon tae yon kirk yard,
It lies low anent ta sin;
An' I'll chap upo' them ane by ane,
Sae weel's the wardle may ken.'

5 It fell upon the Yule time,
When the nichts were lang an' dark,
When in it cam' her three bonnie sons
An' their hats clad ower wi' bark.

6 'Whar got ye that, my three bonnie sons,
Upon yer heids sae high?'
'We got this in Paradise,
But there grows nane there for thee.'

7 'Come ben, come ben, my three bonnie sons;
Come ben, and sup wi' me.
For a' my hoose shall sup this nicht,
Fan my three sons are here.

8 'Blaw up the fire, my maidens a',
Bring water fae the well;
For a' my hoose shall feast this nicht
Fan my three bonnie sons are hale'.

9 'We winna sup wi' thee, mother,
Nor drink nane o' your wine
. . .
Thoch it cam' fae tap or tawn.

45

10 'But ye'll mak' tae us a lang, lang bed,
    An' ye'll mak' it lang an' neat;
    An' ye'll tak' yere nichtgoon ye aboot,
    An' ye'll lie close doon at wir feet.'

11 It's she has made a lang, lang bed,
    She's made it lang an' neat;
    An' she's ta'en her nichtgoon her aboot,
    An' she's lain close doon at their feet.

12 The cock he crawed a merry mornin',
    An' flapped his wings sae wide,
    Fan the youngest tae the eldest said:
    'Nae langer can we bide.

13 'For the cock he craws a merry mornin',
    An' the wild fools bode the day;
    An' the psalms o' heaven will be sung,
    An' we'll be missed away.

14 'For the cock he craws a merry mornin',
    An' the wild fools bode the day;
    An' the gates o' heaven will be shut,
    An' we'll be missed away.

15 She's flowen atween them an' the door
    Like ony a baited bear,
    But they've a' three flawn ower her heid
    Like the wild fools o' the air.

16 'Fareweel, fareweel, wir mother dear,
    Fareweel tae barn an' byre,
    An' fare ye weel, wir little sister,
    That wis stayin' i' the hoose the streen.'

grammarye: grammar.
anent ta sin: against the sun.
chap upo' them: knock on them (? the tombstones).
wardle: world.

bark: most versions have 'birk' (birch), a tree often associated with death, the grave and the other world.
Come ben: come inside.
Fan: when.

tawn: spigot (?)

the wild fools bode the day: the wild fowls announce the day. (The original has 'badeth day', which seems to be an incorrect reading).

Flawn ower her heid: flown over her head.

wir mother: our mother.

the streen: last evening.

Line 3, verse 9, is wanting in the original.

A mother sends her three sons away to school, and later receives news of their deaths. She yearns to see them again, and in due course they appear; but their stay is all too brief, since ghostly visitors are bound to depart, like the spirit of Hamlet's father, at dawn. 'Nothing that we have is more profoundly affecting,' wrote Child (his no. 79), of the version in Scott's Minstrelsy of the Scottish Border. *The one given here was collected in the north-east of Scotland in the 1920s.*

16   Cold Blows the Wind

Twelve months after his death, the ghost of a young man rises from the grave to rebuke his true-love for her excessive grief. She craves one last kiss, but the ghost explains that it would be fatal for her to kiss him. Somewhat paradoxically, he then confronts her with a series of riddles which she must solve, or follow him to the grave. According to Baring-Gould, the belief here is 'that if a woman has plighted her oath to a man, she is bound to him after he is dead, and that he can claim her to follow him into the world of spirits, unless she can redeem herself by solving riddles he sets her' (Songs of the West, 1905, Notes, p. 3). Professor Child believed that we have this ballad 'only in an imperfect form'. Baring-Gould's unique text, collated by him from two versions, of about 1828 and 1889 respectively, might well approximate to a more 'perfect' form.

'Cold blows the wind to - night, sweet-heart, Cold are the drops __ of __ rain. __ The ve - ry first __ love that e - ver I __ had, In green - wood he __ was __ slain. __

47

2 I'll do as much for my true love
  As any young woman may;
  I'll sit and mourn above his grave,
  A twelvemonth and a day.

3 A twelvemonth and a day being up,
  The ghost began to speak:
  'Why sit you here by my graveside,
  And will not let me sleep?

4 'O, think upon the garden, love,
  Where you and I did walk.
  The fairest flower that blossomed there
  Is withered on the stalk.'

5 'The stalk will bear no leaves, sweetheart;
  The flower will never return,
  And my true love is dead, is dead,
  And I do nought but mourn.'

6 'What is it that you want of me,
  And will not let me sleep?
  Your salten tears they trickle down,
  And wet my winding sheet.'

7 'What is it that I want of thee,
  O, what of thee in thy grave?
  A kiss from off thy clay-cold lips,
  And that is all I crave.'

8 'Cold are my lips in death, sweetheart;
  My breath is earthy strong.
  If you do touch my clay-cold lips
  Your time will not be long.'

9 'Cold though your lips in death, sweetheart,
  One kiss is all I crave.
  I care not if I kiss but thee
  That I should share thy grave.'

10 'Go fetch me a light from dungeon deep,
   Wring water from a stone;
   And likewise milk from a maiden's breast,
   Which never babe hath none.'

11 She stroke a light from out of a flint,
   An ice-bell pressèd she;
   She pressed the milk from a Johnniswort,
   And so she did all three.

12 'Now if you were not true in word
   As now I know you be,
   I'd tear you as the withered leaves
   Are torn from off the tree.'

13 Now I have mourned upon his grave
   A twelvemonth and a day;
   I'll set my sail before the wind,
   So waft me far away.

Ice-bell: icicle.
Johnniswort: perhaps this is a local name for Milkwort (Sun Spurge; otherwise known as Mamma's Milk and Virgin Mary's Nipple), which exudes milk, albeit poisonous. St John's Wort gives not white but red juice.

17   The Lover's Ghost

A young man's night visit to his beloved is brought to an end by dawn, when joy in pleasure mingles with sorrow at parting. How much more poignant the emotion when the visitor proves to be a ghost returning from the other world for a brief period, also terminated by cock-crow (whence 'The Grey Cock', a common title for the ballad). Here, very unusually, the revenant is a woman, rather than a man. Perhaps the motif has come from another ballad, 'Fair Margaret and Sweet William' (Child no. 74). The scholar, Hugh Shields, has reservations about our version of 'The Lover's Ghost,' which was first published in 1909 by his fellow-countryman, Patrick Joyce, who learned it as a boy: 'I wonder whether, in publishing it from memory, he did not 'rethink' it a little. The first verse has no trace of ancient style: one would say the work of some post-romantic rhymer of moderate ability. Now, atrocious thought, the editor had a brother [Robert Dwyer Joyce] who responds exactly to this description. I have searched the MSS, the collections, without finding anything which permits us to attribute the verse to either one' ('Une Alba dans la Poésie Populaire Anglaise?' in Revue des Langues Romanes, 1971, pp. 461–75; my translation). Whatever the truth may be, the ballad has continued to hold the interest of singers, and has even turned up in the New World in versions close to that of Patrick Joyce.

2 'Oh, my pretty, pretty cock, oh, my handsome little cock,
  I pray you will not crow before day;
  And your comb shall be made of the very beaten gold,
  And your wings of the silver so grey.'
  But, oh, this pretty cock, this handsome little cock,
  He crew loud a full hour too soon:
  'Oh, my true love,' she said, 'it is time for me to part,
  It is now the going down of the moon.'

3 'And where is your bed, my dearest dear?' he said,
  'And where are your white holland sheets?
  And where are the maidens, my dearest love,' he said,
  'That wait on you while you are asleep?'
  'The clay is my bed, my dearest dear,' she said,
  'The shroud is my white holland sheet;
  The worms and the creeping things are my waiting maids,
  To wait on me whilst I am asleep.'

The Holland Handkerchief

The underlying theme here is that of the dead fiancé coming to claim his living bride. Professor Child disapproved of this ballad ('it would be classed with the vulgar prodigies printed for hawkers to sell'), but grudgingly printed a seventeenth-century broadside version, under the title of 'The Suffolk Miracle', because 'in a blurred, enfeebled and disfigured shape, it is the representative in England of one of the most remarkable tales and one of the most impressive and beautiful ballads of the European continent'. Despite Child's reservations, the ballad continues to cause a marked frisson *in the listener, which is perhaps why W. B. Yeats was attracted to it. This version comes from Packie Byrne, an Irish singer born in 1917.*

2 Many young men to court her came,
   But none of them could her favour gain
   Till there came one of low degree,
   And above them all she fancied he.

3 But when her father he became to know
   That his lovely daughter loved this young man so,
   Over fifty miles he sent her away
   All to deprive her of her wedding day.

4 One night as she lay in her bedroom
   Her love appeared from out the gloom;
   He touched her hand and to her did say:
   'Arise, my darling, and come away.'

5 'Twas with this young man she got on behind,
   And they rode swifter than any wind;
   They rode on for an hour or more,
   Till he cries, 'My darling, my head feels sore.'

6 A holland handkerchief she then drew out,
   And with it wrapped his aching head about.
   She kissed his lips and these words did say:
   'My love, you're colder than any clay.'

7 When they arrived at her father's gate,
   He said, 'Get down, love, the hour is late.
   Get down, get down, love, and go to bed,
   And I'll see this gallant horse is groomed and fed.'

8 And when she rapped at her father's hall,
   'Who's that? Who's that?' her own father called.
   ' 'Tis I, dear father. Did you send for me
   By such a messenger?' – naming he.

9 'Oh, no, dear daughter, that can never be;
   Your words are false and you lie to me,
   For on yon mountain your young man died,
   And in yon green meadow his body lies.'

10 The truth then to know this maiden brave,
   And with her friends they exposed the grave
   Where lay her young man, though nine months dead,
   With a holland handkerchief around his head.

11 Woe to all parents, as I say still,
   Who rob young lovers of their own will;
   For once their promises and vows they give,
   They never can recall them back whilst they live.

19   The Cruel Ship's Carpenter

Promising marriage, a carpenter seduces a woman. When she becomes pregnant, he murders her, and joins the navy as a ship's carpenter. After the crew see the ghosts of the woman and her baby, the carpenter confesses to the murder, and, 'raving distracted', dies. This is the gist of the thirty-three verses of a seventeenth-century broadside ballad, 'The Gosport Tragedy, or the Perjured Ship Carpenter', versions of which remained popular until recent years. Cecil Sharp commented that this was 'one of the few supernatural folk-ballads that are still popular with country singers' (1907).

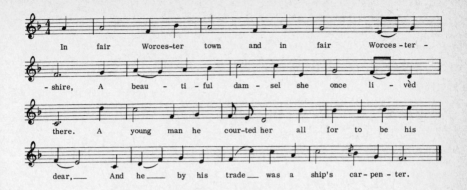

In fair Worces-ter town and in fair Worces-ter-
-shire, A beau-ti-ful dam-sel she once li-vèd
there. A young man he cour-ted her all for to be his
dear,— And he— by his trade— was a ship's car-pen-ter.

2 Early one morning before it was day,
   He went to his Polly, these words he did say:
   'O Polly, O Polly, you must go with me,
   Before we are married my friends for to see.'

3 He led her through woods and through valleys so deep,
   Which caused this poor maiden to sigh and to weep:
   'O Billy, O Billy, you have led me astray
   On purpose my innocent life to betray.

4 'O Billy, O Billy, Oh pardon my life,
   I never will covet for to be your wife;
   I'll travel the whole world to set myself free,
   If you will but pardon my baby and me.'

5 'There's no time for pardon, there's no time to save,
   For all the night long I've been digging your grave.
   Your grave is now open and the spade is standing by';
   Which caused this young damsel to weep and to cry.

6 He covered her up so safe and secure,
   Thinking no one could find her, he was sure.
   Then he went on board to sail the world round,
   Before that the murder could ever be found.

7 Early one morning before it was day,
   The captain he came up and these words he did say:
   'There's a murderer on board and he must be known.
   Our ship is in mourning, we cannot sail on.'

8 Then up steps the first man, 'I'm sure it's not me';
Then up steps the second, 'I'm sure it's not me.'
Then up steps bold William to stamp and to swear:
'I'm sure it's not me, sir, I vow and declare.'

9 Now as he was turning from the captain with speed,
He met with his Polly, which made his heart bleed.
She ripped and she tore him, she tore him in three,
Because that he murdered her baby and she.

20   The Cruel Mother

*Like many another ballad rich in folklore, this has a feeling of ancient
solemnity, though we can trace it no further back than the seventeenth century,
when it appeared as 'The Duke's Daughter's Cruelty: or the Wonderful
Apparition of two Infants whom she Murther'd and Buried in a Forrest, for to
hide her Shame'. The version given here was 'sung by Eliza Wharton and
brothers, children of gipsies, habitually travelling in North Shropshire and
Staffordshire, 13th July, 1885'.*

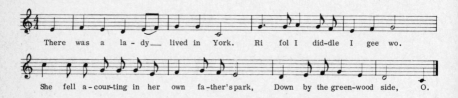

There was a la-dy__ lived in York. Ri fol I did-dle I gee wo.

She fell a-cour-ting in her own fa-ther's park, Down by the green-wood side, O.

2 She leaned her back against the stile [thorn],
There she had two pretty babes born.

3 And she had nothing to lap 'em in,
But she had a penknife sharp and keen.

4 [She did not care if they felt the smart];
There she stabbed them right through the heart.

5 She wiped the penknife in the sludge;
The more she wiped it, the more the blood showed.

54

6 As she was walking in her own father's park, [hall]
    She saw two pretty babes playing with a ball.

7 'Pretty babes, pretty babes, if you were mine,
    I'd dress you up in silks so fine.'

8 'Dear mother, dear mother, [when we were thine],
    You dressed us not in silks so fine.

9 'Here we go to the heavens high;
    You'll go to bad [hell] when you do die.'

in her own father's park: some versions have 'with her own father's clerk', which
    explains why the children are unwanted.
She leaned her back . . . . : ancient and primitive posture for child-bearing
lap: wrap.

21 Molly Bawn

*Instead of punishment, a ghost here brings pardon. The mysterious death of a
woman in the guise of a swan has profound reverberations. It recalls the death
of Procris in classical antiquity and the swan maidens of northern mythology.
Like no. 18, this is another item from the repertoire of Packie Byrne, which
can be heard on his record,* Songs of a Donegal Man *(Topic 12TS257,
1975).*

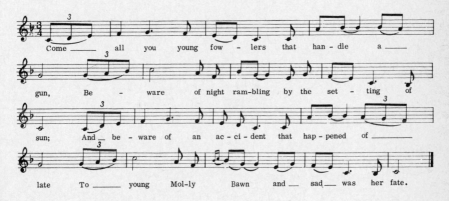

55

2 She was going to her uncle's when a shower came on:
  She went under a green bush the shower to shun.
  With her white apron round her, he took her for a swan,
  But a–hush and a–sigh, it was his own Molly Bawn.

3 He ran home to his father with his gun in his hand,
  Saying, 'Father, dear father, I have shot Molly Bawn.
  I have shot that fair damsel; I have taken the life
  Of the one I intended to take as my wife.

4 'She was going to her uncle's when a shower came on:
  She went under a green bush the shower to shun.
  With her white apron round her, I took her for a swan.
  Oh, father, will I be forgiven for the loss of that swan?'

5 'Oh, Johnny, my Johnny, do not run away,
  Do not leave your own country till your trial day;
  Don't leave your own country till your trial comes on,
  For you'll never be convicted for the loss of a swan.'

6 The night before Molly's funeral her ghost did appear,
  Saying, 'Mother, dear mother, young Johnny is clear.
  I was going to my uncle's when a shower came on:
  I went under a green bush the shower to shun.
  With my white apron round me, he took me for a swan.
  Won't you tell him he's forgiven by his own Molly Bawn?'

7 All the girls of this country are all very glad
  Since the pride of Glen Alla, Molly Bawn, is now dead;
  And the girls of this country, put them all in a row,
  Molly Bawn would shine above them like a mountain of
    snow.

22   **The Grey Selkie**

*There are many traditional tales, especially in northern latitudes, about seals
assuming human form. Here a seal ('selkie') who is 'a man upon the land'
fathers a child, but both father and son are subsequently shot, while in their seal
guise. This version of the ballad was collected as recently as 1970–72 by Alan*

Bruford, who comments that it 'may have been based on a tale that had been told in Norse, even on a Norse ballad, but as we have it it was launched into and carried down on a Scots stream of tradition', starting in Orkney 'probably not much before the beginning of the seventeenth century' ('The Grey Selkie', in Scottish Studies, *vol. 18, 1974, p. 77).*

2 Now it happened one night
  As this fair maid lay fast asleep
  That in there came a grey selkie
  And laid himself down at her bed feet,

3 Crying, 'Awake, awake, my pretty maid,
  For thy babe's father's sitting at thy bed feet.

4 'For I'm a man upon the land,
  A selkie in the sea,
  And I do come from the Wast'ard o' Hoy,
  Which wise men do call Sule Skerrie.

5 'My name it is good Hyne Malair:
  I earn my livin' by the sea,
  An' when I'm far from ev'ry shore
  It's then I am in Sule Skerrie.'

6 'Oh what a fate, what a weary fate,
  What a weary fate's been laid for me,
  That a selkie should come from the Wast'ard o' Hoy
  To the Norway lands to have a babe with me.'

7 'Oh I will wed thee with a ring,
  With a ring, my dear, I'll wed with thee.'
  'Thou may wed thu's weds with whom thou wilt,
  But I'm sure thou'll ne'er wed none wi' me.'

8 'Then thou shalt nurse thy little wee son
   For seven long years upon thy knee;
   And at the end of seven years
   I'll come an' pay thy nurse's fee.'

9 It's oh, she's nursed her little wee son
   For seven years upon her knee;
   And he's come back a gay gentleman
   With a coffer of gold and white monie.

10 She says, 'I'll wed thee with a ring,
   With a ring, my dear, I'll wed with thee.'
   'Thou may wed thee's weds with whom thou wilt,
   I'm sure thou'll ne'er wed none wi' me.

11 'But you will get a gunner good,
   And aye a good gunner he'll be,
   And he'll gaeng out on a May morning
   And he'll shoot the son and the grey selkie.'

(So he took the son away, and . . .)

12 'I'll put a gold chain about his neck,
   [An'a gey good gold chain it'll be]
   That if ever he comes to the Norway lands,
   It's oh, well knowèd he may be.'

13 And oh, she got a gunner good,
   And aye a good gunner was he,
   And he gaed out one May morning
   An' he shot the son and the grey selkie.

(Then he returned and showed her this wonderful thing that
        he'd found, the gold chain on the selkie's neck . . .)

14 'Oh you have shot good Hyne Malair,
   And oh, he was right kind to me.'
   She gied a sigh, sobbed aince or twice,
   And then her tender hert did brak in three.

Hoy: one of the Orkney Isles.
Thou may wed thu's weds: thou mayst go and wed thee.
The words in round brackets were spoken.

58

A series of magical metamorphoses helps in the escape from a pursuer, unless the pursuer has even stronger sorcery at his disposal (as here). In tale and song, the theme is known all over Europe, but ballad versions are extremely rare in Britain: only three examples (two with tunes) have ever turned up. I give here a previously unpublished version (A), together with the earliest known text (B), which comes from Peter Buchan's Ancient Ballads and Songs of the North of Scotland *(1828), and was described by Child as 'a base-born cousin of a pretty ballad'.*

A   1   The smith he stood in his smithy door,
              An' she cam' by the door,
              Could hardly stand for pride.
              The smith he cried:

Chorus   'Bide, lassie, bide,'
              An' aye he bade her bide,
              'An' be a brookie smith's wife,
              An' that will lay your pride.'

2 She became a ship, a ship,
   An' sailed upon the sea,
   An' he became a mariner,
   An' aboard o' her gaed he.

brookie: grimy.
girdle: griddle.
make: match.

duke: duck.
peel: pool.
dreel: rough handling.

B

1 The lady stands in her bower door
   As straight as willow wand;
   The blacksmith stood a little forebye
   Wi' hammer in his hand.

2 'Weel may ye dress ye, lady fair,
   Into your robes o' red;
   Before the morn at this same time,
   I'll gain your maidenhead.'

3 'Awa', awa', ye coal-black smith,
   Wou'd ye do me the wrang
   To think to gain my maidenhead
   That I hae kept sae lang?'

4 Then she has hadden up her hand,
   And she sware by the mold:
   'I wu'dna be a blacksmith's wife
   For the full o' a chest o' gold.

5 'I'd rather I were dead and gone
   And my body laid in grave,
   Ere a rusty stock o' coal-black smith
   My maidenhead should have.'

6 But he has hadden up his hand
   And he sware by the mass:
   'I'll cause ye be my light leman
   For the hauf o' that and less.

      'O bide, lady, bide.'
      And he bade her bide:
      'The rusty smith your leman shall be
      For a' your muckle pride.'

60

7 Then she became a turtle dow
  To fly up in the air,
  And he became another dow
  And they flew pair and pair.
    O bide, lady, bide, etc.

8 She turn'd hersell into an eel
  To swim into yon burn,
  And he became a speckled trout
  To gie the eel a turn.
    O bide, lady, bide, etc.

9 Then she became a duck, a duck,
  To puddle in a peel,
  And he became a rose-kaim'd drake
  To gie the duck a dreel.
    O bide, lady, bide, etc.

10 She turn'd hersell into a hare
  To rin upon youn hill,
  And he became a gude greyhound
  And boldly he did fill.
    O bide, lady, bide, etc.

11 Then she became a gay grey mare
  And stood in yonder slack,
  And he became a gilt saddle
  And sat upon her back.

    Was she was wae, he held her sae,
    And still he bade her bide:
    The rusty smith her leman was
    For a' her muckle pride.

12 Then she became a het girdle
  And he became a cake,
  And a' the ways she turn'd hersell
  The blacksmith was her make.
    Was she was wae, etc.

13 She turn'd hersell into a ship
   To sail out ower the flood,
   He ca'd a nail intill her tail
   And syne the ship she stood.
       Was she was wae, etc.

14 Then she became a silken plaid
   And stretched upon a bed,
   And he became a green covering
   And gain'd her maidenhead,
       Was she was wae, etc.

forebye: aside.   *rose-kaim'd*: with a red comb.
hadden: held.   *fill*: fulfil.
mold: earth.   *slack*: hollow,
light leman: wanton lover.   *wae*: woeful.
hauf: half.   *het girdle*: hot griddle.
dow: dove.   *syne*: then.

24   The Maid on the Shore

A sea captain with ulterior motives persuades a young woman to board his ship. However, she sings him and his crew to sleep, helps herself to silver, gold and 'costely' ware, and thumbs her nose from the shore. Earlier versions have the maiden as a mermaid, which may explain her power to charm the sailors to sleep.

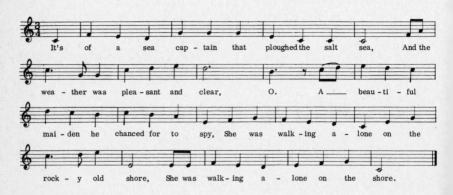

It's of a sea cap-tain that ploughed the salt sea, And the
wea-ther was plea-sant and clear, O. A___ beau-ti-ful
mai-den he chanced for to spy, She was walk-ing a-lone on the
rock-y old shore, She was walk-ing a-lone on the shore.

2 The sailors did hoist out a very long boat,
  And straight for the shore they did steer, O,
  Saying, 'Ma'am, if you please, will you enter on board,
  And view a fine cargo of costely ware,
  And view a fine cargo of ware?'

3 And when they arrived alongside of the ship
  The captain her ordered a chair, O,
  Saying, 'First you shall lie in my arms all this night,
  And then I'll hand you to my jolly old crew,
  And then I'll hand you to my crew.'

4 She sat herself down in the stern of the ship,
  And the weather was pleasant and clear, O.
  Then she sang so neat, so sweet and complete,
  She sang sailors and captain right off to sleep,
  She sang sailors and captain to sleep.

5 She's robbed them of silver, she's robbed them of gold,
  She's robbed them of costely ware, O;
  And the captain's broadsword she took for an oar,
  And she's paddled away for the rocky old shore,
  She's paddled away for the shore.

6 'Oh, were my men drunk, or were my men mad,
  Or were my men drownèd in care, O,
  When they let her escape, which made us all sad?'
  And the sailors all wished she was there, O, there,
  And the sailors all wished she was there.

7 He lowered himself down in the stern of the boat,
  And away for the shore they did steer, O.
  She saluted the captain as well as the crew,
  Saying, 'I'm a maiden once more on the rocky old shore,
  I'm a maiden once more on the shore.'

As Katharine Briggs has said, this ballad, in its fuller versions, 'is a compendium of Scottish fairy beliefs', such as 'the carrying away of anyone who is unconscious of fairy ground, the transformations of mortals to fairies when they are kidnapped, the tiend to Hell, the disenchantment through various transformations, finally confirmed by the putting on of a mortal garment' (A Dictionary of British Folk-Tales, Routledge, 1970, Part A, Vol. 1, p. 502). The ballad was mentioned in Wedderburn's Complaynt of Scotland (1549), but the earliest printing was a fragment in Herd's Ancient and Modern Scottish Songs, Heroic Ballads, &c, which appeared in 1776. The best-known version is perhaps the one communicated by Robert Burns in 1792 to the editor of the Scots Musical Museum. The set given here was recorded in Glasgow as recently as 1974 from a traveller, Betsy Johnston, who can be heard singing it on The Muckle Sangs (Tangent Records TNGM 119/D, 1975).

2 For she kiltit up her petticoats,
   It's up to them she ran;
   And when she came to the merry green woods
   She pulled those branches down, my dear,
   She pulled those branches down.

3 For it's there she spied a gentleman
   Coming through the wood to her side.
   'Oh it's who gave you leave, oh, my dear,
   To pull those branches down, my dear,
   It's who gave you, oh, leave?'

'Oh, please stay the day with me, dad.'
But as the brave miner went forth to his work,
He heard this appeal from his lad.

3 Whilst waiting with his mates to descend,
  He could not vanquish his fears.
  He returned home again to his wife and his child:
  Those words seemd to ring in his ears.
  And ere the day ended the pit was on fire,
  And a score of great men lost their lives;
  The scene it then changed and the top of the mine
  Was surrounded by sweethearts and wives.

'Don't go down in the mine, dad' is a remark which has long had traditional currency. Rejoinders are usually laconic: 'There's plenty of coal on top', or 'The bottom's fallen out of it'. It is not clear whether the saying preceded the ballad, or otherwise. Bad omens are profoundly disturbing to men such as fishermen and miners, and the collier turning back because of his son's dream rings true. According to the singer, Mrs Lucy Woodall (1899–1979) the ballad used to be sung after pit disasters. It was written by one J. R. Lincoln, and first appeared in print in America (United Mine Workers' Journal, 7 February 1911), though it achieved wide popularity in this country.

27

The Well below the Valley

This is Child's 'Maid and the Palmer' (his no. 21). In earlier versions the 'gentleman' of verse 1 is a palmer (pilgrim), or Jesus himself, meeting the woman of Samaria. The painful theme of incest may account for the ballad's extreme rarity – in English at least, though it is not uncommon in other European languages. Indeed, Child has only two versions in English, the most recent being a fragment recalled by Sir Walter Scott. Miraculously, however, it turned up, as ballads do, on the lips of an illiterate travelling man of County Roscommon, in 1969. Tom Munnelly was the collector, and the singer, John Reilly (c.1926–1970), 'one of God's gentry', can be heard on The Bonny Green Tree *(Topic 12TS359, 1978).*

2 'My cup it is an overflow,
   And if I do stoop I may fall in.'

3 'Well, if your true love was passing by,
   You'd fill him a drink if he got dry.'

4 She swore by grass and swore by corn
   That her true love was never born.
   'I say, fair maiden, you've swore in wrong.'

5 'Well, if you're a man of that noble fame,
   You'll tell to me the father of them.'

6 'Two of them by your father dear.

7 'Two more of them came by your uncle Dan.

8 'Another one by your brother, John.'

9 'Well, if you're a man of the noble fame,
   You'll tell to me what happened then.'

10 'There was two o' them buried by the kitchen fire.

11 'Two more o' them buried by the stable door.

12 'The other was buried by the well.'

13 'Well, if you're a man of the noble fame
   You'll tell to me what will happen mysel'.'

14 'You'll be seven long years a-ringin' a bell.

15 'You'll be seven more a-portin' in hell.'

16 'I'll be seven long years a-ringin' the bell,
   But the Lord above might save my soul
   From portin' in hell.'

father of them: a verse omitted in this version runs: ' "Peace, fair maid, you are
   forsworn./Nine children you have borne" '.
portin': being a porter.

A Scots Entertainment.

28

The Cherry Tree Carol

When Jo - seph was an old man, An __ old man was __ he, He __ wed - ded our __ Ma - ry, the Queen of Ga - li - lee.

Var.(a)

2 And when he had a-wedded her and at home had her
    brought,
Mary proved with child, but Joseph knew her not.

3 Then Joseph and Mary was a-walking in the grove;
They saw cherries and berries as red as any rose.

4 When Joseph and Mary were in the garden green
They saw cherries and berries that was fitted to be seen.

5 And Mary said to Joseph in words meek and mild:
  'Pick me some cherries, Joseph, for I am with child.'

6 Then Joseph spoke to Mary in words so unkind:
  'Let him pluck thee cherries, Mary, who brought thee with
     child.'

7 Then Jesus spoke unto the tree from within his mother's
     womb:
  'Bow down, sweet cherry tree, for my mother to have
     some.'

8 Then the highest branches bent as low as Mother Mary's
     knee,
  And she picked of the cherries by one, two and three.

9 Then Mary had a young son which she dandled on her knee,
  And she said to her fair child: 'What will this world be?'

10 'This world,' he said, 'is no other than the stones in the street,
   But the moon, sun and stars shall sail under thy feet.

11 'And I must not be rocked in silver nor gold,
   But in a wood cradle that rocks on the ground.

12 'And I must not be clothed in purple nor pall,
   But be clothed in fair linen, the child is your own.'

*A number of apocryphal narratives about Christ have been preserved in folk
carols. In* Pseudo Matthew *(chapter 20), during Mary and Joseph's flight
into Egypt, the infant Jesus in his mother's lap performs two miracles: he
causes a palm tree to bend low, so that his mother may gather dates, and a
spring of water to well up from its roots so that she might drink. The first
mention of the story in English is in one of the fifteenth-century Coventry
Mysteries. Jesus is here still in his mother's womb, the tree has become the
more homely cherry, and Joseph, instead of merely grumbling about the height
of the tree (which is appropriate to a palm, but not a cherry), utters a tart
comment about the father of Mary's child. The miracle is further enhanced by
the tree's producing fruit out of season. The earliest records of the carol date
from the eighteenth century.*

III
Bid the World Adieu:
Death and Disaster

29   Sir Patrick Spens

It is possible that this ballad stems from a disaster which took place in 1281. Margaret, the daughter of Alexander III, was taken to Norway in August of that year to marry King Eric. Many of the noblemen who accompanied her lost their lives at sea on the way back to Scotland. Child, however (his no. 58), does 'not feel compelled to regard the ballad as historical'. The most important considerations are its great power and beauty.

The first printed version appeared in 1765, in Percy's Reliques. *Ours was collected in the 1920s from a Stonehaven sea captain, James Mason, known as 'Black Jimmie', who had learned it from his father in the 1880s. He had never seen it in print, though it is close to a version in Scott's* Minstrelsy. *He had two tunes, one Ionian (B) and one Aeolian (A), both with fine rhythmic and melodic variation.*

The king sat in Dun—ferm—line toon,

Drink-in' the reid wine; Said, 'Whar'll I get a

jol — ly skip-per To sail this ship o' mine?'

2 It's up an' spak' a nobleman,
Wha sat at the king's richt hand;
It's: 'Ye will get Sir Patrick Spens;
He is walkin' on the sand.'

74

3 The king he wrote a broad letter,
   An' sealed it wi' his hand;
   He sent it to Sir Patrick Spens,
   Wha was walkin' on the sand.

4 The first line that Sir Patrick read,
   Lood, lood laughèd he;
   But the neist line that Sir Patrick read,
   The tear it blint his e'e.

5 'Wha is this that's deen this deed,
   That's telt the king on me,
   To send us oot this time o' the year
   To sail the wintry sea?'

6 'I saw the new moon late last nicht,
   Wi' the auld moon in her airms:
   It's, master dear, if you sail the sea,
   I fear you'll come to harm.'

7 'Be't wind, be't weet, be't snaa or sleet,
   Oor guid ship maun sail the morn,
   To gang ower to Norrawa,
   The king's bride to bring hame.'

8 We hised sail on Monday morn
   Wi' a' the speed we may;
   We landed into Norrowa
   Upon a Wednesday.

9 We hadna been in Norrawa,
   It's weeks but barely twa,
   When that the lords o' Norrawa
   Alood began to say:

10 'Ye Scotsmen spend a' oor queen's gowd,
   An' a' oor queen's fee.'
   'Ye lee, ye lee, ye liars lood,
   Sae lood's I hear ye lee.

11 'For I hae brocht as much money
     As dee wi' my men an' me;
     An' I hae brocht as much reid gowd
     Oot ower the sea wi' me.

12 'Mak ready, mak ready, my merry men a',
     Oor guid ship maun sail the morn.'
     'Whenever you like, my maester dear,
     But I fear a deadly storm.'

13 We hadna sailed a league, a league,
     A league but barely three,
     When the lift grew dark, the wind blew lood,
     An' lood, lood roared the sea.

14 'O, whar'll I get a bonny boy
     To hold my helm in hand,
     Till I gang to the topmast tall
     To see can I find land?'

15 'Here ye'll get a bonny boy
     To hold your helm in hand,
     Till ye gang to oor topmast tall,
     But I fear ye'll ne'er find land.'

16 He hidna gan' a rung, a rung,
     Rungs he gaed but three;
     A voice it shouted up to him:
     'Come doon an' speak wi' me.
     There's a hole in oor ship's side,
     An' the saut sea it comes in.'

17 'Go fetch a web, a silken claith,
     Another o' the twine,
     An' wrap them roon oor goodly ship,
     An' letna the water in.'

18 They fetched a web o' silken claith,
     Another o' the twine,
     An' wrapped them roon oor goodly ship,
     But still the sea cam' in.

19 Ah, laith, laith wis the guid Scots lords
    To weet their cork-heeled sheen,
    But lang o'er a' the play was played
    They wat their hats abeen.

20 Mony was the feather beds
    That floated on the faem,
    An' mony was the guid lords' sons
    That never mair cam' hame.

21 Lang, lang may the maidens sit
    Wi' their fans enti their hands,
    A-waitin' for Sir Patrick Spens
    Comin' sailin' to the land.

22 And lang, lang may the ladies sit
    Wi' their gowd kames in their hair,
    A-waitin' for their husbands dear,
    For them they'll never see mair.

23 But three miles off Aberdeen
    Ye'll get fifty fadoms deep,
    An' there ye'll find Sir Patrick Spens
    Wi' the guid lords at his feet.

Dunfermline: in Fife; once a favourite residence of the kings of Scotland.
blint his e'e: blinded his eye.
deen: done.
Norrawa: Norway.
lee: lie.
lift: sky.
sheen: shoon (shoes).
They wat their hats abeen: they wet their hats above (they were in water over the tops of their heads).

feather beds: the image of so domestic an object as a feather bed floating in the sea conveys a powerful feeling of desolation. However, the truth is more prosaic: from earliest times sailors used feather beds, partly because they were comfortable, but also because the feathers' extreme buoyancy made them excellent life-rafts.
faem: foam, sea.
kames: combs.

There is a tradition that this ballad was inspired by an event at Exton Hall, Rutland, in the early eighteenth century. The owner's daughter, Catherine Noel, aged eighteen, got into a large chest during a game of hide and seek, or, as another story has it, a performance of Romeo and Juliet. *She was unable to re-open the lid, and was suffocated before she could be released.*

The ballad, written by T. H. Bayley and Sir Henry Bishop in the early 1830s, was popular in Victorian drawing rooms, but was also taken up by traditional singers, and printed on street ballads.

2 'I'm weary of dancing now,' she cried,
  'Here, tarry a moment – I'll hide – I'll hide;
  And Lovell, be sure thou'rt the first to trace
  The clue to my secret hiding place.'
  Away she ran and her friends began
  Each tower to search, each nook to scan;
  And young Lovell cried, 'Oh, where doest thou hide?
  I am lonely without thee, my own dear bride.'

3 They sought her that night and they sought her next day,
  They sought her in vain till a week passed away;
  In the highest, the lowest, the loneliest spot,
  Young Lovell sought wildly but found her not.
  Then years flew by, and their grief at last

Was told as a sorrowful tale of the past;
And when Lovell appeared the children cried:
'See the old man weeps for his fairy bride.'

4 At length an oak chest that had long lain hid
Was found in the castle; they raised the lid,
And a skeleton form lay mouldering there,
In the bridal wreath of that lady fair.
Oh, sad was her fate – in sportive jest
She hid from her lord in the old oak chest;
It closed with a spring, and her bridal bloom
Lay withering there in a living tomb.

31   Lord Thomas

Attracted presumably by her wealth, Lord Thomas agrees to marry a mysterious 'brown girl', despite his love for Ellinor. Somewhat foolishly, he invites Ellinor to the wedding, with tragic consequences.

The earliest printed copy of the ballad, which may originally have been a minstrel composition, dates from between 1663 and 1685. This Shropshire version, taken down in 1872, is virtually identical, though longer by three verses. Such growth is very unusual, for ballads usually seem to shrink with the passage of time.

Lord Thomas he was a bold fo-re-ster,
Cha-sing of the king's deer; Fair El-li-nor was a
fine wo-man And Lord Thomas he lo-vèd her dear.

2 ['Come riddle my riddle, dear mother,' he said,
'And riddle us both as one,
Whether I shall marry fair Ellinor,
And let the brown girl alone.'

3 'The brown girl she has got houses and lands,
　And fair Ellinor she has got none;
　Therefore I charge you on my blessing
　To bring me the brown girl home.']

4 It happenèd on a high holiday,
　As many another beside,
　Lord Thomas he went unto fair Ellinor
　That should have been his sweet bride.

5 [But when he came to fair Ellinor's bower,
　He knocked there at the ring;
　But who was so ready as fair Ellinor
　For to let Lord Thomas in.]

6 'What news, what news, Lord Thomas?' she said,
　'What news have you brought unto me?'
　'I am come to bid thee to my wedding,
　And that is bad news unto thee.'

7 'O God forbid,' fair Ellinor cried,
　'That ever such thing should be done.
　I thought to ha' bin the bride my own sel',
　And thee to ha' bin the bridegroom.

8 ['Come riddle my riddle, dear mother,' she said,
　'And riddle it all in one;
　Whether I shall go to Lord Thomas's wedding,
　Or whether I shall tarry at home.'

9 'There's many that are your friends, daughter,
　And many that are your foe;
　Therefore I charge you on my blessing,
　To Lord Thomas's wedding don't go.'

10 'There's many that are my friends, mother,
　If a thousand more were my foe,
　Betide my life, betide my death,
　To Lord Thomas's wedding I'll go.']

11 She dressèd herself in rich attire,
    Her merry men all in green;
    In every town that she rode through
    They took her to be some queen.

12 And when that she raught to Lord Thomas's door,
    So boldly she tirled at the pin;
    O who was so ready as Lord Thomas
    For to let fair Ellinor in?

13 He took her by the lily-white hand,
    He led her through the hall;
    He took her into the drawing room,
    And fixed her above them all.

14 ['Is this your bride?' fair Ellin, she said,
    'Methinks she looks wondrous brown;
    Thou mightest have had as fair a woman
    As ever trod on the ground.'

15 'Despise her not, fair Ellin,' he said,
    Despite her not now unto me;
    For better I love thy little finger
    Than all her whole body.']

16 The brown girl had a knife in her hand,
    It was both keen and sharp;
    And 'twixt the long ribs and the short
    She prickèd fair Ellinor's heart.

17 'O what is the matter?' Lord Thomas he says,
    'Methinks you look wondrous wan,
    Which you used to have as fair a colour
    As ever the sun shone on.'

18 'O are you blind, Lord Thomas?' she says,
    'Or cannot you very well see?
    O cannot you see my own heart's blood
    Run trickling down to my knee?'

19 Lord Thomas having a sword in his hand,
   It was both keen and small,
   He took off the brown girl's head
   And threw it against the wall.

20 He sticked the haft against the floor,
   The point against his own heart.
   O never so soon did three lovers meet,
   And never so soon did part.

21 Lord Thomas was buried in the lower chancèl,
   Fair Ellinor in the higher;
   Out of Lord Thomas there grew a wild rose,
   And out of her a briar.

22 They grew so high, they grew so wide,
   They raught to the chancel top,
   And when that they could grow no higher,
   They knit of a true lover's knot.

raught: reached.

32   **Barbara Allen**

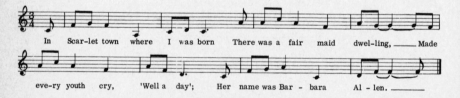

In Scar-let town where I was born There was a fair maid dwel-ling, ____ Made eve-ry youth cry, 'Well a day'; Her name was Bar - bara Al - len. ____

2 Was in the merry month of May,
   When green buds they were swelling,
   Young Johnny Grove on his death-bed lay
   For the love of Barbara Allen.

3 He sent one of his servant men
   To the place where she was dwelling,
   Saying, 'My master's ill and sends for you,
   If your name be Barbara Allen.'

4 'Look up, look up, at my bed-head,
   You'll see a watch-chain hanging;
   Take both my watch and my diamond ring,
   Give them to Barbara Allen.

5 'Look down, look down, at my bed-foot,
   You'll see a basin standing,
   Which is full of tears – and as many more
   Will be shed for Barbara Allen.'

6 Whe he was dead and lay in his grave
   Her heart was filled with sorrow:
   'Oh, mother, mother, make my bed,
   For I shall die tomorrow.

7 'Oh, father, father, dig my grave,
   Dig it both deep and narrow;
   For as my true love died yesterday,
   Then I shall die tomorrow.'

Barbara Allen is indifferent to Johnny Grove, who dies of love for her. She is then filled with remorse, and dies herself. The plot is unconvincing, but the ballad has held a place in men's affections for more than three hundred years. During that time, the feelings of Samuel Pepys and Oliver Goldsmith have been much quoted and widely shared. Pepys heard the actress, Mrs Knipp: 'In perfect pleasure I was to hear her sing, and especially her little Scotch song of Barbary Allen' (1666). Goldsmith heard a humbler singer: 'The music of the finest singer is dissonance to what I felt when an old dairymaid sung me into tears with "Johnny Armstrong's Last Goodnight", or "The Cruelty of Barbara Allen" ' (1765).

Andrew Lammie

'This is a homely ditty', says Child, 'but the gentleness and fidelity of Annie under the brutal behaviour of her family are genuinely pathetic, and justify the remarkable popularity which the ballad has enjoyed in the north of Scotland.' It seems reasonably sure that the ballad has some basis in reality. The ruin of the Mill of Tifty still exists in the glen of Fyvie, about half a mile from the castle, which has the figure of a trumpeter on one of the turrets. Annie was Agnes Smith, whose headstone in Fyvie churchyard shows that she died in 1673. Andrew Lammie, too, seems to have existed, though in the final analysis the ballad has a 'numinous confluence of exploit and dream, of myth and reality'. The phrase is by Hamish Henderson who, with Peter Cooke, recorded this version in 1974 from Sheila MacGregor.

2 Her bloom was like the springin' flower
   That hails the rosy mornin',
   And her innocence and graceful mien
   Her beauteous face adornin'.

3 Noo her hair was fair and her eyes were blue,
   And her cheeks as red as roses;
   And her countenance was fair tae view,
   And they ca'ed her bonny Annie.

4 Noo Lord Fyvie had a trumpeter
   Wha's name was Andra Lammie,
   And he had the airt for tae gain the hairt
   O' the Mill of Tifty's Annie.

5 Noo her mother cried her tae the door,
   Sayin', 'Come here to me, my Annie.
   Did e'er ye see a prettier man
   Than the trumpeter o' Fyvie?'

6 Oh but naethin' she said, but sighin' sair,
   'Twas alas for bonny Annie,
   For she durstnae own that her hairt was won
   By the trumpeter o' Fyvie.

7 And at nicht when all went tae their beds,
   A' slept fu' soond but Annie;
   Love so oppressed her tender breast,
   And love will waste her body.

8 'Oh love comes in to my bedside,
   And love will lie beyond me;
   Love so oppressed my tender breast,
   And love will waste my body.'

9 'My love I go tae Edinburgh town,
   An' for a while maun leave thee.'
   'Oh but I'll be deid afore ye come back
   In the green kirkyaird o' Fyvie.'

10 So her faither struck her wondrous sore,
   An' also did her mother;
   And her sisters also took their score,
   But woe be tae her brother.

11 Her brother struck her wondrous sore
   Wi' cruel strokes and many,
   And he broke her back owre the temple-stane,
   Aye, the temple-stane o' Fyvie.

12 'Oh mother dear, please make my bed,
   And lay my face tae Fyvie,
   For I will lie and I will die
   For my dear Andra Lammie.'

13 Noo when Andra hame fae Edinburgh came
   Wi' muckle grief and sorrow:
   'My love she died for me last night,
   So I'll die for her tomorrow.'

34 Lord Gregory

The heartless reception of another Annie and its disastrous consequences make this ballad deeply moving. It was widely known by the first half of the eighteenth century, and remained in oral circulation until the twentieth. Both Robert Burns and John Clare based poems on it.

'O wha will lace my shoes sae small? An' wha will glove my hand? Or wha will lace my middle sae jimp With my new made linen band?

2 'Wha will trim my yellow hair
With my new siller kame?
An' wha will father my young son
Till Lord Gregory comes hame?'

3 'Your father will lace your shoes sae small;
Your mother will glove your hand;
Your sister will lace your middle sae jimp
With your new made linen band.

4 'Your brother will trim your yellow hair
With a new made siller kame;
An' the king o' heaven will father your son
Till Lord Gregory comes hame.'

5 'But I will get a bonnie boat,
An' I will sail the sea,
For I maun gang to Lord Gregory,
Since he canna come hame to me.'

6 She has gotten a bonnie boat,
An' sailed upon the main;
She langèd to see her ain true love,
Since he could nae come hame.

7 'O row your boat, my mariners,
An' bring me to the land,
For yonder I see my love's castle
Close by the saut sea strand.'

8 She's taen her young son in her airms,
   An' to the door she's gane,
   An' lang she knocked an' sair she ca'ed,
   But answer she got nane.

9 'O open the door, Lord Gregory,
   O open an' lat me in,
   For the wind blaws through my yellow hair,
   An' I'm shiverin' to the chin.'

10 'Awa, awa, ye wile woman,
   Some ill death may ye dee;
   Ye're but some witch or wile warlock
   Or mermaid o' the sea.'

11 'I'm neither witch nor wile warlock,
   Nor mermaid o' the sea;
   But I'm fair Annie o' Rough Royal,
   O open the door to me.'

12 'Gin ye be Annie o' Rough Royal,
   As I trust ye canna be,
   Now come tell me o' the love tokens
   That passed between you an' me.'

13 'O dinna ye mind, Lord Gregory,
   When ye sat at the wine,
   Ye changed the rings fae our fingers?
   An' I can show ye thine.

14 'For yours was good an' very good,
   But aye the best was mine;
   For yours was o' the good red gold,
   But mine the diamonds fine.

15 'Don't ye mind, Lord Gregory,
   By bonnie Irwine side,
   When first I owned that virgin love
   I lang, lang had denied?

16 'O don't ye mind, Lord Gregory,
　　When in my father's ha',
　　'Twas there ye got your will o' me,
　　An' that was worst o' a'?'

17 'Awa, awa, ye wile woman,
　　For here ye sanna win in;
　　Gae drown ye in the ragin' sea,
　　Or hang on the gallows pin.'

18 When the cock did craw an' the day did daw,
　　An' the sun began to peep,
　　Then up did rise Lord Gregory,
　　An' sair, sair did he weep.

19 'I dreamed a dream, my mither dear,
　　The thought o't gars me greet;
　　I dreamed fair Annie o' Rough Royal
　　Lay caul deid at my feet.'

20 'Gin it be for Annie o' Rough Royal
　　That ye mak a' this din,
　　She stood a' last night at our door,
　　But I think I letna her in.'

21 'O wae betide ye, ill woman,
　　Some ill death may ye dee,
　　That ye wadna hae latten poor Annie in,
　　Or else hae wauken'd me.'

22 He's gane down to yon sea shore
　　As fast as he could fare:
　　He saw fair Annie in her boat,
　　An' the wind it tossed her sair.

23 'Hey bonnie Annie, an' how bonnie Annie,
　　O Annie, winna ye bide?' –
　　But aye the mair bonnie Annie he cried,
　　The rougher grew the tide.

24 'Hey bonnie Annie, an' how bonnie Annie,
   O winna ye speak to me?' –
   But aye the mair bonnie Annie he cried,
   The rougher grew the sea.

25 The wind blew loud an' the sea grew rough,
   An' the boat was dashed on shore;
   Fair Annie floats upon the sea,
   But her young son rose no more.

26 Lord Gregory tore his yellow hair,
   An' made a heavy moan;
   Fair Annie's corpse lay at his feet,
   But his bonnie young son was gone.

27 First he kissed her cherry cheeks
   An' next he kissed her chin,
   An' saftly pressed her rosy lips
   That there was not breath within.

28 'O wae betide ye, cruel mother,
   An ill death may ye dee,
   For ye turned my true love fae my door,
   When she cam sae far to me.'

jimp: slender.
kame: comb.
wile: vile.

dinna ye mind: don't you remember.
gars me greet: make me weep.
fare: travel.

35   The Betrayed Maiden

'Love Overthrown. The Young Man's Misery; And the Maids Ruine; Being a true Relation, How a beautiful Herefordshire Damsel . . . was, by her Mistress, sold to Virginia; and of the great Lamentation her Disconsolate Lover makes for her': thus a seventeenth-century ballad in the Pepys Collection, which continued to be sung on both sides of the Atlantic until recent years. The text given here is from a broadside printed by Johnny Pitts at his Toy and Marble Warehouse, Seven Dials, in the early nineteenth century.

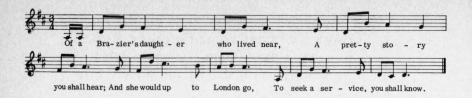

Of a Bra-zier's daught-er who lived near, A pret-ty sto-ry you shall hear; And she would up to London go, To seek a ser-vice, you shall know.

2 Her master had one only son,
   Sweet Betsy's heart was fairly won,
   For Betsy being so very fair
   She drew his heart in a fatal snare.

3 One Sunday night he took his time,
   Unto sweet Betsy he told his mind.
   Swearing by all the powers above,
   ' 'Tis you, sweet Betsy, 'tis you I love.'

4 His mother happening for to hear,
   Which threw her in a fatal snare,
   For soon she contrived sweet Betsy away
   For a slave in the province of Virginia.

5 'Betsy, Betsy, pack up your cloaths,
   For I must see what the country shews,
   You must go with me a day or two
   Some of our relations there for to view.'

6 The rode till they came to a sea town
   Where ships were sailing in the Down,
   Quickly a captain there was found,
   Unto Virginia they were bound.

7 Both hired a boat along side they went,
   Sweet Betsy rode in sad discontent,
   For now sweet Betsy's upon the salt wave,
   Sweet Betsy's gone for an arrant slave.

8 A few days after she returned again,
   'You are welcome, mother,' says the son,
   'But where is Betsy, tell me I pray,
   That she behind so long doth stay?'

90

9 'O son, O son, I plainly see,
　How great your love is for pretty Betsy,
　Of all such thoughts you must refrain,
　Since Betsy's sailing over the watery main.'

10 'We would rather see our son lie dead,
　Than with a servant girl to wed,'
　His father spoke most scornfully,
　'It will bring disgrace to our family.'

11 Four days after the son fell bad,
　No kind of music could make him glad,
　He sighed and slumbered, and often cried,
　' 'Tis for you, sweet Betsy, for you I died.'

12 A few days after the son was dead,
　They wrung their hands and shook each head,
　Saying, 'Would our son but rise again,
　We would send for Betsy over the main.'

36   The Swan Swims So Bonny

The bones of a corpse serve to make a musical instrument, which sings by itself to reveal the identity of a murderer, the victim's older sister. This powerful theme has an atavistic quality, and the ballad was probably already ancient when it was first printed, in 1656. It is known throughout Europe, and has also been found in Africa and America.

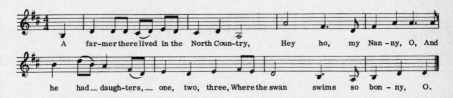

A far-mer there lived in the North Coun-try, Hey ho, my Nan-ny, O, And he had daugh-ters, one, two, three, Where the swan swims so bon-ny, O.

2 These daughters they walked by the river's brim,
　And the eldest pushed the youngest in.

91

3 'Oh sister, oh sister, pray lend me your hand,
  And I will give you house and land.'

4 'I'll neither give you hand nor glove,
  Unless you give me your own true love.'

5 Sometimes she sank, sometimes she swam,
  Until she came to the miller's dam.

6 The miller's daughter, being dressed in red,
  She went for some water to make her bread.

7 'Oh father, oh daddy, here swims a swan,
  And it's very like to a gentlewoman.'

8 They laid her on the bank to dry;
  There came a harper passing by.

9 He made a harp of her breast-bone,
  And the harp began to play alone.

10 He made harp-pins of her fingers so fair,
   He made his harp-strings of her golden hair.

11 He brought it to her father's hall;
   There was the court assembled all.

12 He laid the harp upon a stone,
   And straight it began to play alone.

13 'Oh yonder sits my father, the king,
   And yonder sits my mother, the queen.

14 'And yonder sits my brother, Hugh,
   And by him my William, sweet and true.

15 'And there does sit my false sister, Anne,
   Who drowned me for the sake of a man.'

37   The Sheffield Apprentice

*The fury of a woman scorned has been proverbial ever since Potiphar's wife.
Here, the runaway 'prentice is not as fortunate as Joseph, and he ends on the
'gallows tree'. This late eighteenth-century ballad has more than a whiff of
class consciousness, with disaster caused by the venom of the rich lady rejected
for a servant girl. It remained current on both sides of the Atlantic for over a
hundred and fifty years, almost invariably retaining the title and reference to
Sheffield. The tune used here is often associated with 'The Manchester
Angel', another tale of lost love.*

I was brought up in Shef - field, but not of high de - gree; ___ My
pa - rents do - ted on me, they had no child but me; ___ I
rol - led in much plea - sure, where -'er my fan - cy led, ___ Till
I was bound ap - pren - tice, then all my joys they fled. ___

2 I did not like my master – he did not use me well –
   And took a resolution not long with him to dwell.
   Unknown to my poor parents, from him I ran away,
   And steered my course for London. Oh, cursed be that day.

3 A handsome, lovely damsel, from Holland, she was there,
   She offered me great wages to serve her for a year;
   And after great persuasion with her I did agree
   To go with her to Holland, which proved my destiny.

4 I had not been in Holland years but two or three,
   Until my lovely mistress grew very fond of me;
   She said her gold and silver, her houses and her land,
   If I'd consent to marry her should be at my command.

5 I said, 'Dear, honoured lady, I cannot wed you both,
   And lately I have promised and made a solemn oath
   To wed with none but Polly, your pretty chambermaid;
   Excuse me, my dear mistress, for she has my heart betrayed.'

6 Then in an angry passion away from me she's gone,
   Swearing to be avenged on me before 'twas long;
   For she was so perplexed she could not be my wife
   That soon she laid a project to take away my life.

7 One day as I was walking all in the garden green,
   The flowers they were springing delightful to be seen;
   A gold ring from her finger as she was passing by
   She slipped into my pocket, and for it I must die.

8 Now in a few days after in haste then I was called
   Before a dreadful justice to answer for the fault;
   Though long I pleaded innocence it was of no avail,
   She swore so sore against me that I was sent to jail.

9 My mistress swore I robbed her, which ne'er was my intent;
   Because I would not marry her, she did it from contempt.
   From that place of confinement she brought me to the tree,
   Oh, woe be to my mistress for she has ruined me.

10 All you that stand around me my wretched fate to see,
   Don't glory in my downfall but rather pity me.
   Don't blame me, I am innocent; I bid the world adieu –
   Farewell, my pretty Polly, I die for love of you.

38   Little Montgrove and Lady Barclay

*'I sing Musgrove, and for the Chevy Chace no lark comes near me': thus a
character in Davenant's play,* The Wits *(1636), using the more normal name
for the doomed lover. The ballad's widespread popularity in the early seventeenth century is further attested by other references, including one as early as
c. 1611, in Beaumont and Fletcher's* Knight of the Burning Pestle. *The
earliest registered of several broadside printings was in 1630. Passionate,
adulterous love, a warning tragically ignored, both lovers dying: such a tale
could hardly fail to grip. This version has one unique variation of plot:
whereas Lord Barclay (normally Barnard) elsewhere kills both lovers, here
Lady Barclay ends her own life.*

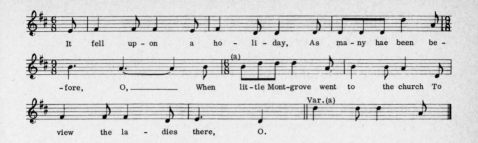

It fell up-on a ho-li-day, As ma-ny hae been be-fore, O, _____ When lit-tle Mont-grove went to the church To view the la-dies there, O.

2 Some come in wi' high, high heids,
   And some as black's a coal, O,
   Till in it cam' Lord Barclay's lady,
   The floor oot ower them a', O.

3 'I hae a boor in Billsbury,
   Well built wi' stone and lime, O,
   And you and I, little Montgrove,
   Will sleep ae night therein, O.'

4 'To sleep ae nicht wi' you, lady,
   It wid breed muckle strife, O,
   For I ken you by the ring o' your fingers,
   That you're Lord Barclay's wife, O.'

5 'I care as much for Lord Barnard
   Hie turin o' a stra', O;
   I could see as muckle o' his heart's bleed
   As ae sword would lat go, O.'

6 They hadna weel lien doon,
   Nor wis they weel asleep, O,
   Fan up it starts the little foot page:
   His wis close at their bed feet, O.

7 'Heal weel, heal weel, my little foot page,
   Heal weel, heal weel on me;
   Gin ye keep this a' a bit o' a secret
   Atween my lord an' me O.'

8 I carena for your money,' he says,
   'Nor yet for nean o' your fee, O,

But I hope this nicht afore I sleep
My ain guid lord to see, O.'

9 He twa fit crap an' twa fit leap,
Till he went tae the wa', O;
And he is on tae his lord's boor
As fast as he could dra', O.

10 It's fan he cam' till his lord's boor door,
Says, 'Rise and lat me in, O;
For little Montgrove's in bed wi' your lady,
To sleep till they think time, O.'

11 'An' that be a lee, ye little foot page,
That ye dee tell to me, O,
The highest tree in Billsbury
High hangit ye shall be, O.

12 'Gin that be true, ye little foot page,
That ye dee tell to me, O;
I hae an only dochter fair:
Your wedded wife she'll be, O.

13 'Ye'll rise, ye'll rise, my merry young men,
Ye'll rise an' gae wi' me, O;
An' ye'll rise, ye'll rise, my merry young men,
We're bound for Billsbury, O.'

14 He pit his horn enti his mouth,
He's blown it lood and shrill, O:
'Gin ye be in bed wi' Lord Barclay's lady,
It's time ye were o'er the hill, O.'

15 It's 'Waken, waken, lady,' he says,
'An' hear the trumpet soun', O';
Says, 'Gin ye be in bed wi' Lord Barclay's lady
It's time ye were oot o' the toun, O.'

16 'Lie doon, lie doon, ye little Montgrove,
An' keep me fae the cald, O;
That's but ane o' my lord's shepherds,
Drawin' his sheepies fae the fald, O.'

17 They had nae well lien doon,
   Nor was they weel asleep, O,
   Fan up it starts him Lord Barclay,
   Close by their bed fit, O.

18 'How d'ye like my blankets, Montgrove,
   Or how d'ye like my sheets, O?
   Or how d'ye like the lady fair
   That lies in your airms an' sleeps, O?'

19 It's 'Weel like I your blankets, my lord,
   An' better like I your sheets, O;
   But woe be to this wild, wicked woman
   That lies in my airms an' sleeps, O.'

20 'Rise up, rise up, ye little Montgrove,
   An' pit your clothing on, O.
   I widna hae it telt in the land
   That I'd slain a naked man, O.'

21 Up it starts him, little Montgrove,
   An' he could hardly stand, O.
   'Ochone, alas,' said little Montgrove,
   'I've neither sword nor wand, O.'

22 'I hae twa in my scabbard
   An' ye shall get the ane, O.
   I'll tak' the warst, gi'e ye the best;
   We'll facht till they gae dean, O.'

23 The first stroke that little Montgrove gae,
   Oh dear, but he struck sair, O;
   But the first stroke Lord Barnard gae,
   Little Montgrove ne'er gi'ed mair, O.

24 It's up the lady's ta'en the sword
   An' stripped it through the strae, O,
   An' through and through her fair body
   She gart cold iron gae, O.

25 There wis nae pity for that twa lovers
In the room where they lay deed, O;
The pity was for the bonny baby
That was welterin' amon' the blood, O.

26 There wis nae pity for that twa lovers
In the room where they lay slain, O;
But the pity wis a' for Lord Barclay,
For that nicht he's gane brain, O.

floor: flower.
boor: bower.
Fan: when.
Heal: conceal, hide.
Gin: if.
He twa fit . . . : he made two creeps and made two leaps.
lee: lie.
He pit his horn: not Lord Barclay, of course, but, as we know from other versions, one of his retinue who is trying to warn the lovers.
Ochone: woe is me.
wand: staff.
facht till they gae dean: fight till they go down, are put down.
sair: sore.
gart cald iron gae: made cold iron go.
brain: mad.

39   Green and Yellow

The ancient ballad of 'Lord Randal' or 'Henry, My Son' was still well enough known in the late nineteenth century to inspire this music-hall parody.

'Where have you been all day, Hen - ry, my son?
Where have you been all day, my pret - ty one?'
'In the woods, dear mo - ther. In the woods, dear mo - ther. Oh,
mo - ther be quick, 'cause I want to be sick, And lay me down and die.'

2 'What did you do in the woods today, Henry, my boy?
What did you do in the woods today, my saveloy?'
'Ate, dear mother. Ate, dear mother.
Oh, mother, be quick, 'cause I want to be sick, and lay me
down and die.'

98

3 'What did you eat in the woods today, Henry, my son?
  What did you eat in the woods today, my currant bun?'
  'Eels, dear mother. Eels, dear mother.
  Oh, mother, be quick, 'cause I want to be sick, and lay me
    down and die.'

4 'What colour were them eels, Henry, my boy?
  What colour were them eels, my pride and joy?'
  'Green and yeller. Green and yeller.
  Oh, mother, be quick, 'cause I want to be sick, and lay me
    down and die.'

5 'Them weren't eels, them was snakes, Henry, my son.
  Them weren't eels, them was snakes, my pretty one.'
  'Ugh, dear mother. Ugh, dear mother.
  Oh, mother, be quick, 'cause I want to be sick, and lay me
    down and die.'

6 'What colour flowers d'you want on your grave, Henry, my
    boy?
  What colour flowers d'you want on your grave, my pride and
    joy?'
  'Green and yeller. Green and yeller.
  Oh, mother, be quick 'cause I want to be sick, and lay me
    down and die.'

40 The Poor Little Fisher Boy

Down in the low-lands a poor boy did wan-der,
Down in the low-lands a poor boy did roam. By his
friends he was ne-glect-ed, he looked so de-ject-ed:
'I'm a poor lit-tle fish-er-boy, so far a-way from home.'

2 'Oh, where is my cottage, oh, where is my father?
Alas, they're all gone, which causes me to roam.
Mother died on her pillow, my father in the billows,'
Cried the poor little fisherman's boy, so far away from home.

3 'Oh, bitter was the night, and so loudly roared the thunder,
The lightning did flash and our ship was overcome.
The mast I soon clasped round till I reached my native ground;
In the deep I left my father, so far away from home.

4 'I waited on the beach while around me rolled the water,
I waited on the beach, but, alas, no father came.
So now I am a ranger, exposed to every danger,'
Cried the poor little fisherman's boy, so far away from home.

5 A lady she heard him, she opened her window,
And into her house she bid him to come.
The tears fell from her eyes as she listened to the mournful
      cries
Of the poor little fisherman's boy, so far away from home.

6 She begged of her father to find him employment,
She begged of her father no more to let him roam.
Her father said: 'Don't grieve thee, the boy he shall not leave
      me;
Poor boy, I will relieve thee, so far away from home.'

7 Many years he laboured to please his noble master;
Many years he laboured; in time, a man became.
Now he tells the stranger of the hardships and the danger
Of a poor little fisherman's boy, so far away from home.

The Victorians loved a tear-jerker, and this tale of charity to an orphan had many parallels, with the beneficiaries usually being seafarers – sailors and even smugglers – but also soldiers, and even mechanics. The tune is a variant of the well-known 'All Round My Hat'.

Rambling Robin

Youthful folly and the passage of time are enough to produce 'grief and woe' for the eponymous Robin of this charming little ballad.

When first from my child-hood I came to a man, ——— The na - tion to ram - ble round I soon be - gan; ——— For a wan - der - ing thought it came in - to my mind, ——— So they christened me Ram - bling Ro - bin, O, ——— So they christened me Ram - bling Ro - bin. ———

2 O'er hills and o'er mountains I used for to go;
I've slept in the woods in the frost and the snow.
No anxiety ever came into my mind,
So contented was Rambling Robin.

3 The wind and the rain beat against me quite cold;
My parents at home they were both very old.
My father did weep and my mother did cry
For the loss of their Rambling Robin.

4 When sixteen long years they were over and past,
My poor mother's sorrows were ended at last;
My father the nation did range through and through,
In search of his Rambling Robin.

5 Now when my past folly was run to an end
To my own native village I soon did attend;
The neighbours all told me my parents were dead,
With the thoughts of their Rambling Robin.

6 Now where shall I wander or where shall I go?
I'm sorely oppressed with grief and with woe;
I'll wander no more till the day that I die:
There's an end to Rambling Robin.

IV
An Awful Story:
Deeds of Daring

42   The Lambton Worm

In the Middle Ages the Lambtons lived in a castle near the village of Penshaw in County Durham. The story goes that the young heir caught a strange-looking worm in the River Wear and threw it in a well. During Lambton's long absence on a crusade in the Holy Land the worm grew to a tremendous size and terrorized the whole district. Attempts to kill it failed because whenever the monster was cut in two, the halves joined together again. On his return home, acting on the advice of a witch, Lambton succeeded in killing the worm by covering his armour with razors and standing in the river. When the worm wrapped itself round him it was cut into pieces, which were carried away by the current and prevented from joining up again. The price of the witch's advice was a promise that Lambton would kill the first creature to meet him after the battle. He had arranged that his father should release a dog, but the old man forgot to do so, and rushed out himself. Naturally, Lambton refused to kill him, but in so doing incurred the witch's curse that his successors would die violently – which seems to have come true. The song, originally composed in the 1860s, treats the story in jocular fashion, and omits the curse. It is still popular in the north-east.

One Sun-day morn young Lamb-ton went a - fish-ing in the Weor; He
catched a fish u - pon his heuk he thowt looked var - ry queor, But
whatn a kind o' fish it was, young Lamb-ton could - na tell: He
wad - dent fash ter tak it yairm, so he hoyed it in the well.

Chorus

Whisht, lads, haad yer gobs, Ah'll tell yer all an aa - ful sto - ry,
Whisht, lads, haad yer gobs, Ah'll tell yer a - boot the worm.

2 Then Lambton felt inclined ter gan an' fight in foreign wars,
He joined a troop o' knights that cared for neether wounds nor
scars.
So off he went to Palestine, where queor things him befel,
And varry soon forgot aboot the queor worm in the well.

3 This aaful worm, it graad an' graad, it graad an aaful size,
Wi' a greet big heed an' a greet big gob, an' greet big goggly
eyes;
An' when at neet it wandered oot ter pick up bits o' news,
If it felt dry upon the road it milked a dozen coos.

4 This fearful beast would often feast on calves an' lambs an'
sheep,
And swally'd bits o' bairns alive when they lay doon ter sleep;
An' when it'd eaten aal it could an' it'd had its fill,
It'd craal away an' lap its tail ten times roond Pensha Hill.

5 The news o' this most aaful beast an' its queor gannins on
Soon crossed the seas, got to the ears o' bold and brave Sir
John;
So yairm he came an' catched the worm, an' cut it in three
halves,
Soon put a stop tiv its eatin' bairns an' lambs an' sheep an'
calves.

103

6 So now yer knaa how aal the folks on both sides of the Weor
   Lost lots o' sleep an' lots o' sheep, an' lived in mortal feor;
   So let's have one ter bold Sir John who saved the bairns from
      harm,
   Saved sheep an' calves by makin' halves o' the famous
      Lambton Worm.

Last Chorus

Naw, lads, Ah'll haad me gob, that's aal Ah knaa aboot the
   story,
Aboot Sir John an' his clivvor job wi' the famous Lambton
   Worm.

fash: bother.   *hoyed*: threw.
yairm: home.   *whisht*: hush.

43   Dilly-dove

A wild boar is ravaging the district, so a champion sallies forth and kills it. In fuller versions of the ballad, the boar is the creature of a witch, who is killed in her turn. The story is often linked with Bromsgrove in Worcestershire, where the tomb of Sir Humphrey Stafford (who died in 1450) bears a coat of arms which includes a boar's head. This is probably a localization, since the ballad has its roots in medieval romance, and in particular in the poem Sir Eglamour of Artois. *The version given here was collected in Herefordshire in 1909.*

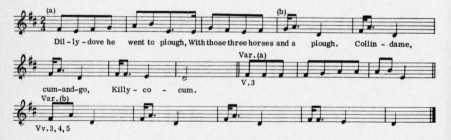

2 Dilly-dove he went to plough,
   And saw a fair maid on a bough.

104

3 He said, 'Fair maid, what makes you sit so high,
   That no young man can come anigh?'

4 'O there's a wild boar in the wood;
   If I come down he'll suck my blood.'

5 'If you'll come down and go with me,
   Both you and I will go and see.'

6 Then he went unto the park,
   And shot the wild boar to his heart.

7 Then he went unto the den,
   And there were bones of forty men.

44   Long John, Old John and Jackie North

The light-hearted ballad of Long John may have started life as a parody of the more intense 'Johnnie Scot' (Child no. 99), though it seems to have survived better, having been collected from oral tradition as recently as the 1950s. Its appeal is further illustrated by this version, a rifacimento *by Martin Carthy of 'Lang Johnny More' (Child no. 251), which he sings on the record,* Because It's Here *(Topic 12TS389, 1979).*

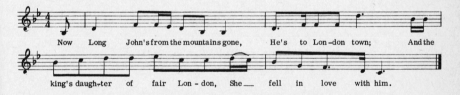

2 Now Long John was a giant born,
   He was fourteen feet in height,
   And the king's daughter she wept for him
   As she laid alone at night.

3 And when the king he heard of this
   An angry man was he;
   Says, 'This mighty man shall stretch the rope
   That hangs on the gallows tree.'

4 So he sent men and cunning men,
  And around him they did creep;
  And they fed him drops of laudanum,
  And they laid him fast asleep.

5 So that when he's awaked out of his sleep
  A sorry man was he,
  With his jaws and hands in iron bands
  And his feet in fetters three.

6 So he's bribed him a servant, Long John,
  He has given him meat and fee,
  To run to his uncle, Old John,
  To come and rescue he.

7 And the first few miles the little boy walked,
  And the next few miles he ran;
  And he run till he come to the broad water,
  Where he laid down and swam.

8 And when he came to the mountain high,
  He cried out aloud;
  There he spied him Jackie North
  With Old John by his side.

9 And there as these two giants stood,
  A grisly sight to see.
  For they were tall as the eagle's call
  And broad as the oaken tree.

10 'Oh, rise, rise, Old John,
  Jackie North, come thee,
  For Long John's in prison strong,
  And hangèd he must be.'

11 So they ran over hill and they ran over dale,
  And they ran over mountain high,
  Till they came down to London town
  At the dawning of the day.

12 They cried: 'Open up your city gates,
   Open at my call.'
   Then they up with their feet and they kicked a hole
   Straight in through London Wall.

13 And they trampled down by Drury Lane –
   The crowd before them ran –
   Till there they spied him, Long John,
   Stood under the gallows pin.

14 They said: 'Is it for murder, is it for rape,
   Is it for robbery?
   For if it's for any heinous crime
   We'll stand and watch you die.'

15 He says: 'Not for murder, not for rape,
   Not for robbery;
   But it's all for the love of a gay lady
   They're here to see me die.'

16 So they took him down from the gallows pin;
   Before the king went they.
   Their armour bright cast such a light
   It fair dazzled his eye.

17 'Good day to you,' cries Jackie North,
   'Good day to you,' cries he;
   'For we have come for your daughter's wedding
   All down from the mountains high.'

18 When the king he seen 'em come
   An angry man was he;
   Cries: 'One of you is dole enough.
   What shall I do with three?

19 'O, cursèd be that serving boy
   The tidings bore away;
   For I do vow and I do swear
   High hangèd he shall be.'

20 'Oh, if you hang this little boy
    The tidings brought to me,
    We three shall come to his burial,
    And paid you'll surely be.'

21 'A priest, a priest,' Long Johnny cries,
    'To join my love and me;
    A priest, a priest,' Long Johnny cries,
    'For married we shall be.'

22 'Oh, take my daughter, Long John,
    My curse upon you fall;
    And take my serving boy also,
    Lest all my city fall.'

23 They've taken the lady by the hand,
    Set her prison free;
    And the drums did beat and the fifes did play:
    They spent the night with glee.

24 And then Long John and Old John,
    Jackie North, all three,
    A freed bride and a serving boy
    Went back to the mountains high,

25 Saying, 'If we'd known what we know now,
    Great ones you like to see;
    We'd have brought our sister Jean of the Side –
    She's twenty feet and three.'

dole: grief.

45   The 'Golden Vanity'

*A courageous deed is recompensed by ingratitude. The tale was first told to the
discredit of Sir Walter Raleigh in a ballad printed in the 1680s. The 'little
ship-boy' was promised both money and Raleigh's oldest daughter, but after
sinking the 'false gally' was offered only the money. 'Then fare you well, you*

*cozening Lord,' was his reply, 'seeing you are not as good as your word.' In
later versions there is a far more gripping end. Raleigh has been forgotten, and
the captain of the ship not only refuses all reward to the boy, but even causes his
death by declining to allow him back on board. The version given here comes
from a Brighton fisherman, Johnny Doughty (born 1903).*

2 'What will you give to me,' asked the little cabin boy,
  If I venture to that Spanish ship, the ship that doth annoy?
  I will wreck the gallalee, you may peace of mind enjoy,
  As we sail by the lowlands low.'

3 The captain said, 'Now with you my lad I'll share
  All my treasure and my wealth; you shall have my daughter
      fair
  If this Spanish ship you nobly sink and ease me of my care,
  As we sail by the lowlands low.'

4 Then boldly the lad he did leap into the sea,
  And an auger very sharp and thin he carried carefully;
  And he swam the mighty billows till he reached the gallalee,
  Where she sank by the lowlands low.

5 Then back to the ship the little hero hied,
  And he begged the crew to haul him up upon the larboard
      side.
  'You can sink for me, you little dog,' the ungrateful captain
      cried,
  'As we sail by the lowlands low.'

Was there ever half a tale so sad
As this tale of the sea,
Where we sailed by the lowlands low?

annoy: harass.

46 Robin Hood and the Bishop of Hereford

Despite its medieval setting, there is no record of this ballad before the early eighteenth century; yet by the mid-nineteenth, according to Chappell, it was the most popular in the whole of the Robin Hood canon. At about that time it was learned by George Stone of Wareham, Dorset, who sang it to H. E. D. Hammond in 1906.

Some— will— talk of bold — Ro-bin Hood, Der-ry der-ry down, And
some of the ba-rons so bold; But I'll tell you how they— served the bi-shop when they
robbed him of his gold. — Der-ry down, hey, der-ry der-ry down.

2 Robin Hood he dressed himself in shepherd's attire,
   And six of his men also;
   And when the bishop did come by
   They round the fire did go.

3 'Oh, we are shepherds,' said bold Robin Hood,
   'And keep sheep all the year;
   And we are resolved to make merry today,
   And to eat of our king's fat deer.'

4 'You are a brave fellow,' said the old bishop,
   'And the king of your doings shall know;
   Therefore make haste and come along with me,
   And before the king you shall go.'

110

5 Robin Hood set his back against an oak,
  And his foot against a thorn;
  And out underneath his shepherd's cloak
  Pulled out his bugle-horn.

6 He put the small end to his mouth,
  And a loud blast he did blow;
  Six score and ten of bold Robin's men
  Came tripping along in a row.

7 'Oh, what is the matter?' said Little John,
  'Oh, why do you blow so hastily?'
  'Oh, the Bishop of Hereford he has come by,
  And a pardon he shall have.'

8 'Here's the bishop,' said bold Robin Hood,
  'No pardon I shall have.'
  'Cut off his head, master,' said Little John,
  'And bundle him into his grave.'

9 'Oh, pardon me, oh, pardon me,' says the bishop,
  'Oh, pardon me, I pray.
  If I had a-known it had been you,
  I'd a-gone some other way.'

10 Robin Hood he took the bishop by the hand,
  And led him to merry Barnsdale,
  And made sup with him that night,
  And drink wine, beer and ale.

11 'Call in the reckoning,' the old bishop said,
  'For I'm sure 'tis going very high,'
  'Give me your purse, master,' said Little John,
  'I'll tell you bye and bye.'

12 Little John he took the bishop's cloak
  And spread it on the ground,
  And out of the bishop's portmanteau
  He pulled five hundred pound.

13 'There's money enough, master,' said Little John,
' 'Tis a comely sight to see;
It makes me in charity with the bishop:
In his heart he don't love me.

14 Little John he took the bishop by the hand,
And he caused the music to play;
And he made the old bishop dance till he sweat,
And he was glad to get so away.

47   Johnnie o'Braidisleys

Much ink has flowed in efforts to fix the true location of ballads such as this, but the real point is not historicity but ethos. Some versions have a happy ending, with Johnnie recovering and being honoured by the king, but they are at variance with the feeling of doomed defiance which pervades the ballad as a whole. No text is extant from earlier than the eighteenth century; the version given here was learned by the singer in about 1860.

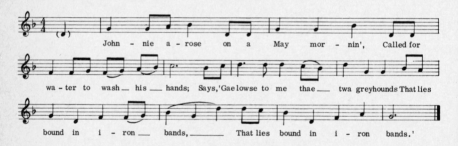

John - nie a - rose on a May mor - nin', Called for wa - ter to wash his hands; Says,'Gae lowse to me thae twa greyhounds That lies bound in i - ron bands, That lies bound in i - ron bands.'

2 When Johnnie's mother she heard o' this,
Her hands wi' dool she wrang;
Says, 'Johnnie, for your venison
To the green woods dinna gang.

3 'We hae plenty o' the white bread,
An' plenty o' the good red wine;
So, Johnnie, for your venison
To the greenwood dinna gang.'

112

4 But Johnnie has breskit his good benbow,
His arrows one by one;
An' he is on to the gay green woods
For to pull the dun deer doon.

5 As he gaed doon through Merriemoss,
An' doon amon' yon scroggs,
'Twas there he spied a dun deer lie
At the back o' the bush o' broom.

6 Johnnie shot, an' the dun deer lap,
He had wounded her in the side,
An' atween the water an' the wood,
An' the greyhounds laid her pride.

7 Johnnie has handled the deer so weel,
Taen oot her liver an' lungs,
An' he has fed the dogs wi' them
As though they'd been yearl's sons.

8 They ate so much o' the raw venison,
An' they drank so much o' the blood,
That Johnnie an' his twa greyhounds
Fell asleep as gin they'd been dead.

9 By there cam' a silly old man,
Some ill death may he dee;
An' he is on to the seven foresters
For to tell what he did see.

10 'What news, what news, ye silly aul' man,
What news hae ye to gie?'
'Nae news, nae news,' said the silly aul' man,
'But what my twa een did see.

11 'As I cam' doon through Merriemoss,
An' doon amon' youn scroggs,
An' the bonniest youth that ever I saw
Lay a-sleepin' atween twa dogs.

113

12 'The coat he bore upon his back
   Was o' the Linkum twine,
   An' the stock he wore aroon his neck
   It was pearl an' precious stone.

13 'The buttons he wore upon his coat
   They were o' the gold so good,
   An' the twa greyhounds that he lay atween,
   An' their mouths were a' dyed wi' blood.'

14 'Twas oot then spak the first forester,
   An angry man was he;
   Says, 'An' this be Johnnie o' Braidisleys,
   My faith, we'll gar him dee.'

15 'Twas oot then spak the second forester,
   His sister's son was he;
   Says, 'An' this be Johnnie o' Braidisleys,
   We'd better let him be.'

16 'Twas oot then spak the seventh forester,
   He was forester ower them a';
   Says, 'An' this be Johnnie o' Braidisleys,
   An' to him an' we'll gang.'

17 The first shots that the foresters fired,
   An' they wounded him in the knee;
   An' the second shots that the foresters fired,
   An' the red blood blinded his ee'.

18 As Johnnie awakened oot o' his sleep,
   An angry man was he;
   Says, 'Ye micht hae waukened me oot o' my sleep
   Ere the red blood blinded me ee'.

19 'Gin my bow prove true as she used to do,
   An' my courage do not fail,
   I'll mak' ye dearly rue that day
   Ye cam' to the Dinspeerhill.'

20 He planted his back against an oak,
   His foot against a stone,
   An' he has shot the seven foresters,
   He has shot them a' but one.

21 He has broken three o' that one's ribs,
   Likewise his collar bone,
   An' he laid him two faul' ower his steed,
   Bade him carry the tidings home.

22 'Noo whaur will I get a bonnie little bird
   That wad sing as I will say,
   That will fly on to my mother's bower,
   An' tell them to tak' Johnnie away?'

23 The starling flew to his mother's bower,
   It whistled an' sang,
   An' aye the owercome o' its sang
   Was 'Johnnie tarries lang'.

24 Some o' them pu'd o' the hawthorn's bush,
   An' some o' the hollin tree,
   An' mony, mony were the men
   At the fetchin' o' young Johnnie.

25 Noo Johnnie's good benbow is broke,
   An' his twa greyhounds they're slain;
   Noo Johnnie sleeps in the Merriemoss,
   An' his huntin' days are done.

26 But woe be to yon silly aul' man,
   An ill death may he dee,
   An' the highest tree in Merriemoss
   Shall be his gallows tree.

lowse: loose.
dool: sorrow.
breskit: strung.
scroggs: bushes.

Linkum twine: Lincoln green.
gar him: make him.
two faul': doubled.
owercome: outcome.

McPherson's Rant

James McPherson's long career of robbery culminated in a reign of terror in the markets of Banff, Elgin and Forres. Apparently under the protection of the Laird of Grant, he and his band of followers would come marching in with a piper at their head. Perhaps he became too powerful for comfort for he was hanged at Banff in 1700, for bearing arms at Keith market. A certain haste to get rid of him is evidenced by the period of only eight days which elapsed between sentence and execution, and there is a tradition that a reprieve failed to arrive in time since the town clock and thus the hour of execution was put forward. McPherson is said to have composed the farewell 'rant' himself, delivered it from the gallows, then broken his fiddle. An instrument which purports to be his has been preserved at the Clan McPherson Museum, Newtonmore, Inverness-shire. This version of the ballad, which Thomas Carlyle found 'wild and stormful', and dwelling 'in ear and mind with strange tenacity' was sung by Jimmy McBeath (1894–1971), who can be heard on Wild Rover No More *(Topic 12T173, 1967). His performance concludes with two of the verses from Robert Burns' reworking of the traditional text.*

2 'There's some cam' here to see me hang't,
   An' some to buy my fiddle;
   But before 'at I do part wi' her
   I'll break her through the middle.'

3 He took the fiddle into both of his hands
   An' he broke it over a stone;
   Says he: 'There's no anither han'll play on thee
   When I am dead and gone.

4 It wis by a woman's treacherous hand
  'At I wis condemned to dee:
  Below a ledge a windae she stood,
  Then a blanket she threw ower me.

5 The laird o' Grant, the Highland sa'nt,
  'At first laid hands on me;
  He played the cause on Peter Broon
  Tae let McPherson dee.

6 Untie these bands from off my hands,
  An' gae bring to me my sword,
  For there's no a man in all Scotland
  But'll brave him at his word.

7 The reprieve was comin' o'er the brig o' Banff
  For tae let McPherson free,
  When they put the clock a quarter before,
  Then hanged him to the tree.

8 I've lived a life o' sturt an' strife;
  I die by treachery.
  O it breaks my heart, I must depart,
  An' live in slavery.

9 Fareweel you life, you sunshine bright,
  And all beneath the skies;
  For in this place I'm ready to:
  McPherson's time tae die.'

sa'nt: saint.   *sturt*: violence.

49   The Draggletail Gipsies

A band of gipsies cast a spell on a lady to make her run away with them. Her husband returns home, discovers that she is gone, and sets off in pursuit. When he catches up, the lady refuses to leave the gipsies, either because she has become genuinely enamoured of her 'gipsy laddy' or that she fatalistically realizes that there is no going back. The last word belongs to her husband, who hangs the gipsies. It is difficult not to connect this dénouement with the hangings of gipsies in Scotland in the early seventeenth century for failing to leave the country, as ordered by the Act of Parliament of 1609, especially as the ballad hero usually has the archetypal gipsy name of Johnny Faa. The earliest texts date from the eighteenth century; later versions, such as this one, collected by Cecil Sharp in Somerset in 1904, omit both the spell at the beginning and the hangings at the end: the heroine has become (to use current jargon) merely a romantic 'drop-out'.

2 This lady come down in a silken gownd,
Put on her Spanish livery O;
Says she, 'This night I'll resign
To follow the draggletail gipsies O.'

3 'Twas late at night when her lord came home
Inquiring for his lady O;
The servants replied on every side:
'She's gone with the draggletail gipsies O.'

4 'Come saddle me my milk-white steed,
Come bridle me my pony, too,
That I might ride and seek for my bride.
She's gone with the draggletail gipsies O.'

5 Then he rode high and he rode low,
He rode through wood and copses, too;
He rode till he came to the woodside,
And there he found his lady O.

6 'What makes you leave your house and land?
What makes you leave your money, too?

What makes you leave your new-wedded lord,
To follow the draggletail gipsies O?'

7 'What care I for house or land?
What care I for my money O?
What care I for my new-wedded lord?
I'll follow the draggletail gipsies O.'

8 'Last night you could lie on a good feather bed,
And into the arms of your Johnny, too;
And now you must ride on the wide open land
Along with the draggletail gipsies O.'

Put on her Spanish livery O: other versions have 'shoes of Spanish leather'.

50   **The Female Sailor**

Stories and songs of female sailors and soldiers (not to speak of highway-men) are legion, and not all are fictional. For example, Charlotte Petrie of Aberdeen shipped aboard the Expedient *at the age of fifteen in 1861 on a voyage from Shields to Palermo: 'During the passage I performed my duties as ordinary seaman, not the least suspicion having arisen among my 'mates' during the voyage; but when in the harbour my sex was discovered and the captain kindly took me to the British Consul' (Sunderland Herald, 8 December 1865). Charlotte Petrie seems to have been merely a tomboy in search of adventure, but Ann Jane Thornton in the song was seeking her true love – the usual motive for female venturers in man's apparel. I do not know whether she really existed, but the song reads at times like a versified news-paper report.*

Good peo - ple give at - ten - tion who now a - round me stand, While I un - fold a cir - cum - stance that does to love be - long; Con - cer - ning of a pret - ty maid who ven - tured, we are told, All a - cross the bri - ny o - cean as a fe - male sai - lor bold.

2 Her name was Ann Jane Thornton, as presently you will hear,
And, as we are informed, she was born in Gloucestershire;
Her father lived in Ireland, respected well, we are told,
But never thought his daughter was a female sailor bold.

3 She was courted by a captain when scarce sixteen years of age,
And to be bound in wedlock this couple did engage;
But the captain had to leave this land, as I will now unfold,
Then she ventured o'er the ocean like a female sailor bold.

4 She dressed herself in sailor's clothes and, overcome with joy,
She with a captain did engage to serve as cabin boy;
And when New York in America this fair maid did behold
She run to seek her lover true, did this female sailor bold.

5 She to her true love's father, she hastened there with speed,
And enquired for employment, but – dreadful news indeed –
Her lover had some time been dead, this pretty maid was told;
Then in agony and sorrow wept the female sailor bold.

6 Some thousands of miles she was from home, from parents
      far away;
She travelled seventy miles through woods in North
      America,
Bereft of friends and kindred, no parents to behold.
'My true love's gone,' in anguish cried the female sailor bold.

7 With pitch and tar her hands were hard, though once like
      velvet soft;
She weighed the anchor, heaved the lead and boldly went
      aloft;
Just one and thirty months she braved the tempest, we are
      told,
And always done her duty, did the female sailor bold.

8 In the month of February, eighteen hundred and thirty-five,
She to the port of London in the *Sarah* did arrive;
Her secret was then discovered and the secret did unfold,
And the captain gazed with wonder on the female sailor bold.

9 This female was examined of course by the Lord Mayor,
   And in all public papers the reasons did appear:
   Why she left her father, her native land she sold,
   To cross the briny ocean as a female sailor bold.

10 It was to seek her lover she sailed across the main;
   Through love she did encounter storm, tempest, wind and
        rain.
   It was love caused all her troubles and hardships, we are told:
   May she rest at home contented now, the female sailor bold.

51   Grace Darling

Grace Darling was a flesh and blood heroine. The rescue which made her famous took place on 6 September 1838. With her father, who was the keeper of the Longstone Lighthouse on the Farne Islands, off Northumberland, she rowed a small boat a mile and back in mountainous seas to rescue survivors from the wreck of the steamer, Forfarshire. *She died four years later, at the age of only 27.*

'Twas on the Longstone Lighthouse there dwelt an English maid, Pure as the air around her, of danger ne'er afraid. One morning just at daybreak a storm-tossed crew she spied, But oh, to try seemed madness, to face the angry tide.

Chorus

She pulled away o'er the rolling sea, over the waters blue. 'Help, help,' you could hear the cry of the shipwrecked crew. Grace had an English heart, and the stormy winds she braved; She pulled away through the splashing spray and the crew she saved.

121

2 There to the rocks was clinging a crew of nine, all told;
Between them and the lighthouse the seas like mountains
   rolled.
Grace cried, 'Come help me, father, to launch the boat,' cries
   she;
Her father said, ' 'Tis madness to race the raging sea.'

3 They murmured a prayer to heaven and then they were afloat;
Between them and destruction were the planks of that fragile
   boat.
Up spoke the maiden's father: 'I believe that doomed are we.'
Up spoke the brave Grace Darling: 'We'll face the raging sea.'

4 They bravely fought the billows and reached the rocks at
   length,
To save those storm-tossed sailors, along with heaven their
   help.
Go, tell the wide world over what English pluck can do,
And sing of brave Grace Darling who boldly saved that crew.

52 The Proud Tailor

*This high-spirited, mock-heroic squib hits a common mark in folklore, the
tailor. One wonders, however, whether it is also legitimate to read it as a satire
on militarism. The ballad is rare: only one full version exists, apart from this
one, which comes from Sam Bennett (1865–1951) of Ilmington,
Warwickshire. However, it is very close to the better-known 'Tailor and
Louse'.*

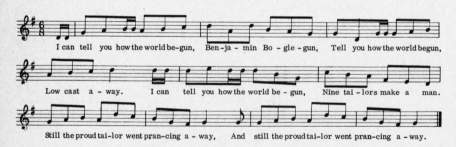

2 The tailor were sat at work (3),
   Picked a louse off his shirt.

3 With his needle he made a sword (3),
  Stabbed the louse on the board.

4 With his bodkin he made a gun (3),
  Shot the louse as he run.

5 With his scissors he made some shears (3),
  Snipped off the louse's ears.

6 With his thimble he made a bell (3),
  Rung the louse into hell.

Low cast away: the other version has 'castors away' (hats off).

53   The Rambling Royal

A great many songs deal with heroism in battle, but here the subject is the daring needed to run away from the army. This forceful tale of protest goes back at least to 1798, when Irish rebels had a version beginning 'I am a real republican, John Wilson is my name'. I would guess that the version given here dates from the 1920s. It came to me from Phil Colclough, who learned it in Liverpool.

Oh, I am a ram - blin' Ro - yal, — from Li - ver - pool I came, — And to my sad mis - for - tune I en - lis - ted in the Ma- - rines. — Being drunk when I en - lis - ted, not know-ing what I'd done, — Un - til my so - ber sen - ses re - turned to me a - gain. —

2 Well, I had a girl in Birkenhead, a true friend, as it seems.
  It broke her heart and made her smart to see me in the
      Marines;
  She said, 'If you desert, young man, as I do hope you may,
  I'll have you in my own bedroom if you should chance to
      stay.'

3 It was at the Chatham Depot the officer gave command
   That me and two of my comrades that night on guard should
      stand.
   The night, being dark and wet and cold, with me did not
      agree,
   So I knocked out a guardroom corporal and ran for my
      liberty.

4 Oh, I rambled all that livelong night until I lost my way,
   And I landed in some farmer's barn and stretched out on the
      hay.
   When I awoke it was no joke for there all at my head
   The sergeant and the officer and two bloody swaddies stood.

5 Well, we had a terrible fight and I damn' near beat them all;
   I made my cowardly comrades in agony to bawl,
   But they locked me in the glasshouse my sorrows to deplore,
   With a man at every window and a man at every door.

6 It was early the very next morning, I paced the guardhouse
      round;
   I jumped out of a window and felled three of them to the
      ground,
   But the provost and his bullies, they was quickly after me,
   But I made my way to Birkenhead and so gained my liberty.

7 Oh, I am a ramblin' Royal, James Cronin is my name;
   I can fight as many officers as you'll find in the Marines.
   I can fight as many Orangemen as ever banged a drum,
   And I'll make 'em run before me like a bullet from a gun.

glasshouse: guardroom (normally means a military prison).
provost: the provost or regimental police sergeant.

54   Erin-go-Bragh

A Scots countryman in Edinburgh gets the better of an officious policeman who harasses him because he thinks him Irish. 'Erin-go-Bragh' (rhyming with braw), means 'Ireland for ever'.

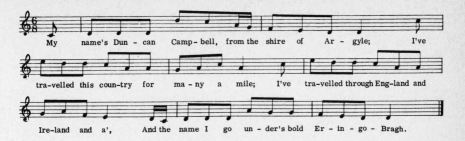

My name's Dun-can Camp-bell, from the shire of Ar-gyle; I've
tra-velled this coun-try for ma-ny a mile; I've tra-velled through Eng-land and
Ire-land and a', And the name I go un-der's bold Er-in-go-Bragh.

2 One night in Auld Reekie as I walked down the street
A saucy policeman by chance I did meet;
He glowered in my face and he gave me some jaw,
Saying, 'When came ye over, bold Erin-go-Bragh?'

3 'I am not a Paddy, though Ireland I've seen,
Nor am I a Paddy, though in Ireland I've been;
But though I were a Paddy that's nothing ava,
There's many a bold hero from Erin-go-Bragh.'

4 'I know you're a Pat by the cut of your hair,
But you all turn Scotchmen as soon's you come here;
You have left your own country for breaking the law –
We are seizing all stragglers from Erin-go-Bragh.'

5 'Though I were a Paddy and you knew it to be true,
Or were I the devil – pray what's it to you?
Were it not for the baton you have in your paw,
I would show you a game played in Erin-go-Bragh.'

6 Then a switch of blackthorn that I held in my fist,
Across his big body I made it to twist;
And the blood from his napper I quickly did draw,
And paid him stock and interest for Erin-go-Bragh.

7 The people came round like a flock of wild geese,
  Crying, 'Stop, stop the rascal, he has killed the police';
  And for every friend I had, I'm sure he had twa –
  It was very tight times with bold Erin-go-Bragh.

8 But I came to a wee boat that sails on the Forth;
  I picked up my all, and I steered for the North.
  Farewell to Auld Reekie, policemen and a' –
  May the devil be with them, says Erin-go-Bragh.

9 Now all you brave fellows that listen to my song,
  I don't give a farthing to where you belong;
  I come from Argyle in the Highlands so braw,
  But I ne'er take it ill when called Erin-go-Bragh.

ava: at all.

126

V
Sentence Passed:
Crime and Punishment

55   **Lambkin**

Lamb - kin, the fi - nest ma - son that — e'er laid a stone, He
built a — lord's man - sion and for pay - ment got none. He —
built it — with - out and he — sealed it — with - in, And he
made a false win - dow for him - self to — get in.

2 His lordship going to London once upon a time,
  The Lambkin thought fit to commit his great crime.
  'I fear the Lambkin,' the lady did say;
  'I fear the Lambkin when your lordship's away.'

3 'I fear not the Lambkin, nor any of his kind,
    When my gates are well barred and my windows pinned
        down.'
    So in stepped the Lambkin in the middle of the night,
    Without coal or candle to show him the light.

4 'Where is his lordship?' then said the Lambkin.
    'He's in London buying pearls,' said the false nurse to him.
    'Where's her ladyship?' said the Lambkin.
    'She's in her chamber sleeping,' says the false nurse to him.

5 'How will I get at her?' says the Lambkin.
    'Stab the baby in the cradle,' says the false nurse to him.
    'It's a pity, it's a pity,' said the Lambkin.
    'No pity, no pity,' says the false nurse to him.

6 So the Lambkin he rocked and the false nurse she sung,
    And with a small pen-knife he dabbed now and then.
    So the Lambkin he rocked and the false nurse she sung,
    And the tearing of the cradle made the blood cold to run.

7 'Please my child, nurse; please him with the keys';
    'He won't be pleased, madam, you may do as you please.'
    'Please my child, nurse, please him with the bell';
    'He won't be pleased, madam, till you come down yoursel'.'

8 'How can I come down, as my candle is out,
    And the room is so dark that I cannot move about?'
    'You have three golden mantles as bright as the sun;
    Throw one of them round you, it will show you light
        down.'

9 As soon as her ladyship entered the stairs,
    So ready was the Lambkin to catch her with his snares.
    'Good morrow, good morrow,' says the Lambkin;
    'Good morrow,' says the lady to him.

10 'Where is his lordship?' says the Lambkin.
    'He's in London buying pearls for my lying-in.'
    'You never will enjoy them,' says the Lambkin;
    'The more is the pity,' says the lady to him.

11 'Spare my life, Lambkin, spare it but one day;
   I will give you as much gold as you can carry away.'
   'If you give me as much gold as I could heap in a sack,
   I could not keep my pen-knife from your lily-white neck.'

12 'Spare my life, Lambkin, spare it but one hour;
   I'll give you my daughter, Bessie, your bride for to be.'
   'Bring down your daughter, Bessie, she's both neat and
        trim,
   With a silver basin to hold your life-blood in.'

13 'Oh, no, no; that, Lambkin, that would never do;
   If you say that, then Bessie will never be for you.
   Bessie, lovely Bessie, stay up in your room.
   Watch for your father coming home, and that will be soon.'

14 Bessie sat watching that cold winter night,
   With her father coming home with his men at daylight.
   'Father, dear father, what kept you so long?
   Your lady is murdered and your own darling son.

15 'There is blood in the kitchen, there is blood in the hall;
   But the blood of my mamma is the worst blood of all.
   For the Lambkin will be hung high up on a tree,
   And the false nurse will be burned, such a villain was she.'

silver basin: there was a superstitious horror of spilling noble blood on the ground.

*Lambkin (or Lammikin, or Rankin, or Long Lonkin), aided by a nursemaid,
kills a noble lady and her child. He is caught by the lord, and executed. English
versions of the ballad give no motive for the ruthless crime, but Scots (and from
those, Irish and American) texts mention – in the first verse – that Lambkin is
a mason who has received no recompense for building a castle. Many attempts
have been made to attach the ballad to a particular locality, or to give it
significance as a covert symbol on the one hand for leprosy, or on the other for
medieval revolt. The terrible story seems more akin to certain nursery tales
which, although they are full of social and linguistic significance, have as their
prime motive the cathartic arousal of terror. The version given here stems from
an old Irish travelling woman of the late nineteenth century, who 'made the
children's flesh creep with this sinister song'.*

56   **Mrs Dyer, the Baby Farmer**

The old ba-by far-mer 'as been ex-e-cu-ted, It's
Chorus: The old ba-by far-mer, the wretch-ed Mrs. Dy-er, At

quite time she was put out of the way. She was a bad wo — man it
the Old Bai-ley her wa-ges is paid. In times long a-go we'd 'a'

is not dis-pu-ted, Not a word in her fa-vour can a-ny-one say.
made a big fy-er, And roast-ed so nice-ly that wi-cked old jade.

2 It seems rather hard to run down a woman,
But this one was hardly a woman at all;
To get a fine living in a way so inhuman,
Crossin' in luxury on poor girls' downfall.

3 Poor girls who fall from the straight path of virtue,
What *could* they do with a child in their arms?
The fault they committed they could not undo,
So the baby was sent to the cruel baby farms.

4 To all these sad crimes there must be an ending;
Secrets like these for ever can't last.
Say as you like, there is no defending
The horrible tales we have heard in the past.

5 What did she think as she stood on the gallows,
Poor little victims in front of her eyes?
Her heart if she had one must have been callous,
The rope round her neck – how quickly time flies.

6 Down through the trap-door quickly disappearing,
The old baby farmer to eternity home;
The sound of her own death bell she was hearing,
Maybe she was sent to the cruel baby farm.

crossin': possibly 'carousing'.

Mrs Dyer and her son-in-law, Arthur Palmer, ran an establishment at
Caversham which was later dubbed a baby farm. They took in and adopted

unwanted infants at fees ranging from ten to a hundred pounds per head. When numbers became a problem, they simply – and insanely – murdered their charges, over forty of them, and dropped their bodies in the Thames. Amidst universal execration, they were hanged, in June, 1896. The tune used here is more commonly associated with 'The Unfortunate Lad' (no. 68).

57   Young Henry Martin

Henry Martin is probably a corruption of Andrew Barton, the name of a Scots pirate who, with his two brothers, was granted letters of marque to attack Portuguese shipping. He became none too particular about the nationality of his victims, and eventually Henry VIII became so infuriated with his depredations that in 1511 he despatched the Lord High Admiral against him. Barton was killed and his ship, Lion, taken. The story was related in some detail – up to 82 verses – in the ballad, 'Sir Andrew Barton', but its descendants, usually called 'Henry Martin', deal only with one episode, originally subsidiary, in which the pirate is successful.

2 The lot it fell out on young Henry Martin,
   The youngest of these brothers three,
   That he should go sailing all on the salt sea, salt sea, salt sea,
   To maintain his two brothers and he.

3 We had not been sailing on a cold winter's morning,
   Three hours before it was day,
   Before we espied a lofty tall ship, a tall ship, a tall ship,
   Coming sailing all on the salt sea.

4 'Hallo, hallo,' cried bold Henry Martin,
'How dare you come sailing so nigh?'
'We're a rich merchant ship bound for old England, England,
England,
Will you please for to let us pass by?'

5 'Oh, no, no, no,' cried bold Henry Martin,
'That never, no, never can be;
For I am turned pirate to rob the salt sea, salt sea, salt sea,
To maintain my two brothers and me.

6 'Take down your top royal, cut away your mainmast,
Come hither in under my lee;
For I will take from you all your flowing gold, flowing gold,
flowing gold,
And return your fair bodies to the sea.'

7 Then broadside and broadside we valiantly fought,
We fought for four hours or more,
Till Henry Martin gave her a dead shot, a dead shot, a dead
shot,
And down to the bottom she goes.

8 Bad news, bad news, you English heroes,
Bad news I have for to tell:
There's one of your rich ships lies sunk off the land, off the
land, off the land,
And all of your merry men drowned.

58   The Bold 'Princess Royal'

*Of all the pirate ballads, this one, in which crime emphatically does not pay, is
perhaps the best known and loved. East Anglian singers are particularly fond
of it, and this version comes from Bob Hart (1892–1978), of Snape, Suffolk.*

'Twas the four-teenth of Fe-bru-a-ry we sailed from the land In the bold *Prin-cess Ro-yal* bound to New-found-land; With — for-ty brave sea-men for a ship's com-pa-ny, And so proud-ly from the east-ward to the west-ward bore she.

2 We scarce had been sailing but days two or three
When a man on the topmast a tall ship did see;
She came bearing down on us just to see what we were,
And under her mizzen strange colours she wore.

3 'Oh, dear,' cried the captain, 'what shall we do now?
Here come a bold pirate to rob us I know.'
'Oh, no,' cried our chief mate, 'that can never be so,
We will shake out our reefs, boys, and from her we'll flow.'

4 Meanwhile the old pirate had come alongside;
With a loud-speaking trumpet: 'Where from you?' he cried.
Our captain being up, he did answer him so:
'We come from fair London and we're bound to Karoo.'

5 'Well, lower your topsails and heave your ship to,
For I have some letters to send home by you.'
In replying to this our captain did say:
'I'm afraid we must leave you and get on our way.'

6 They chased us all night and they chased us all day;
They chased us to windward but ne'er could us stay.
They fired shots after us but none could prevail,
And the bold *Princess Royal* soon shew them her tail.

7 'Thank God,' cried our captain, 'now the pirate is gone,
Go you down to your grog, boys, go you down every one;
Go you down to your grog, my boys, and be of good cheer,
For whilst we have sea room, brave boys, never fear.'

Karoo: often, Peru.

133

Jack Donahue

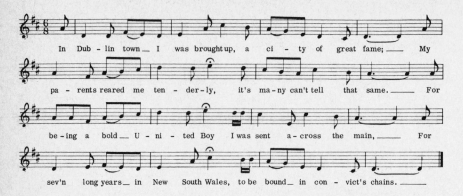

In Dub-lin town_ I was brought up, a ci-ty of great fame; ___ My

pa-rents reared me ten-der-ly, it's ma-ny can't tell that same. ___ For

be-ing a bold_ U-ni-ted Boy I was sent a-cross the main, ___ For

sev'n long years_ in New South Wales, to be bound_ in con-vict's chains. ___

2 I'd been no longer than six months upon the Australian shore,
When I turned out a Fenian boy as I had been before;
There was Mick O'Mara from Underwood and Captain
    Mackie too,
Those were the chief associates of bold Jack Donahue.

3 As O'Donahue was walking out one Sunday afternoon
He little had the notion that his death would be so soon,
When a sergeant of the horse police he charged his carabine
And shouted to O'Donahue to fight or to resign.

4 'To resign to you, you cowardly dog, is a thing I ne'er should
    do,
I'd rather fight with all my might than mercy to you sue;
I'd rather range the wild woods o'er like a wolf or kangaroo,
Before I'd work for government,' cried bold Jack Donahue.

5 Nine rounds the sergeant fired before the fatal ball
Had lodged in the breast of O'Donahue and caused him for to
    fall.
Before he closed his weary eyes he slowly bid adieu,
Saying, 'Good people all, both great and small, say a prayer
    for John Donahue.'

John Donahue was born in Dublin in 1807. At the age of 17 he was sentenced
to transportation for life, and arrived at Sydney aboard the Ann and Amelia
in 1825. Shortly afterwards he bolted, and took to the roads. He was twice

recaptured and sentenced to death, and twice escaped to the bush in the area between Sydney and the Blue Mountains. He was eventually hunted down by troopers in 1830, and killed. His career inspired songs which lasted for well over a century after his death; this one was collected in 1971. 'The Wild Colonial Boy' is another ballad which probably owed its inspiration to Donahue's fame.

60   Heather Jock

'The original of the song – John Ferguson', as Robert Ford puts it, 'lived, moved and had his being in and about Dunblane' [Perthshire] (Vagabond Songs and Ballads of Scotland, 1901, p. 134). He was an incorrigible, though likeable thief and cattle stealer. After being transported to Botany Bay for a term he found his way back, but was then sentenced, in 1812, to transportation for life.

2 Jock kent ilka bore an' bole;
  Could creep through a wee bit hole;
  Quietly pilfer eggs an' cheese,
  Dunts o' bawcon, skeps o' bees;
  Sip the kirn an' steal the butter;
  Nail the hens without a flutter;
  Na'! the watchfu', wily cock
  Durstna craw for Heather Jock.

135

3 Eppie Blaikie lost her gown
   She cost sae dear at borough town;
   Sandy Tamson's Sunday wig
   Left the house to rin the rig;
   Jenny Baxter's blankets a'
   Took a thocht to slip awa':
   E'en the wean's bit printed frock;
   Wha' was thief but Heather Jock?

4 Jock was nae religious youth;
   At the priest he thrawed his mouth.
   He wadna say a grace nor pray,
   But played his pipes on Sabbath day;
   Robbed the kirk o' baan and book.
   Everything wad lift, he took;
   He didna lea' the weather-cock,
   Sic a thief was Heather Jock.

5 Nane wi' Jock could draw a tricker;
   'Mang the muirfowl he was siccar;
   He watched the wild ducks at the springs
   And hanged the hares in hempen strings.
   Blassed the burns and speared the fish;
   Jock had many a dainty dish;
   The best o' muirfowl and blackcock
   Graced the board o' Heather Jock.

6 Keepers catched him on the muir,
   Kickit up an unco stoure;
   Charged him to lay doun his gun,
   Or his nose should delve the grun'.
   Jock slipped doun ahint a hurst,
   Cried, 'Ye swabs, I'll empty't first.'
   They saw his fingers at the lock
   And left the field to Heather Jock.

7 Aften fuddling at the stills,
   Sleepin' sound amang the hills;
   Blazin' heath and cracklin' whins
   Choked his breath and brunt his shins.

136

Up he got in terror vast,
Thocht 'twas doomsday come at last;
Glowerin' dazed thro' fire and smoke,
'I'm in hell,' cried Heather Jock.

8 Nane wi' Jock had ony say
At the neive or cudgel play;
Jock for bolt nor bar e'er stayed
Till ance the jail his courage laid.
Then the judge without delay
Sent him aff to Botany Bay,
And bade him mind the laws he broke,
And never mair play Heather Jock.

9 Jock's bit housie i' the glen
Lies in ruins, but an' ben;
There the maukin safe may rest,
And the muirfowl build her nest.
Ower the sea Jock's herdin' swine,
Glad wi' them on husks to dine;
Sae tak' warnin', honest folk –
Never do like Heather Jock.

croosely: merrily.
swank: agile.
unco: very.
bore an' bole: crevice and recess.
dunts: blows.
skeps: skips (hives).
kirn: churn.
cost: bought.
rin the rig: run the ridge.
wean: baby.

tricker: trigger.
siccar: steady.
Blassed the burns: lit up the streams with blazing torches (in order to spear fish).
stoure: fuss.
ahint a hurst: behind a bank.
lock: of the gun.
neive: fist.
but an' ben: kitchen and parlour.
maukin: hare.

61   The Parson's Peaches

The Norfolk singer, Peter Bellamy, made this ballad from a tale told in the village of Warham, where he was brought up. The tune is a variant of 'The Barley Straw'.

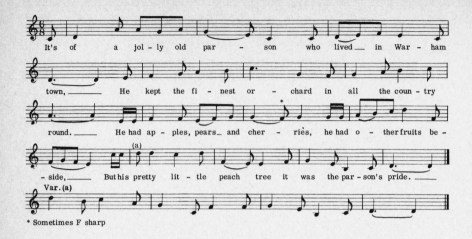

It's of a jol-ly old par - son who lived___ in War - ham town,_____ He kept the fi - nest or - chard in all the coun-try round._____ He had ap - ples, pears_ and cher - ri̇es, he had o - ther fruits be - side,_____ But his pretty lit - tle peach tree it was the par - son's pride._____

(a)

Var. (a)

* Sometimes F sharp

2 He grew this peach tree from a stone, he tended it with care,
   And it made his mouth to water thinking on the fruit she'd
       bear;
   And at last the summer come to pass where the boughs with
       bounty hung,
   But ere the sun had ripened them he found his peaches gone.

3 So he brooded through the winter long till he conceived a plan
   To catch whoe'er had robbed him, be it child or maid or man;
   So he hastened to the good blacksmith who lived just down
       the street,
   Saying, 'Make for me a stout man-trap to catch a burglar's
       feet.'

4 It was a few months after the blacksmith he came round.
   He said, 'Show me where you want your trap and I'll chain it
       to the ground.'
   So to the orchard they repaired, the iron snare to hide,
   And in long grass concealed it with the cruel jaws gaping
       wide.

5 Now it was late in the evening before he went to bed,
   As the parson sat a-drinking a thought come to his head;
   And it's to the orchard he did go for to find if it were true
   That the trap were not set near the gate that the villain must
       come through.

138

6 When he found that this was so, he stood and scratched his
    head,
  Then he moved the engine gingerly into a nettle bed,
  And says he, 'My fruits are ripening but now they'll stay for
    me,
  Because this funny nettle clump lies between the gate and
    tree.'

7 It was round about the midnight hour when all lay sound
    asleep,
  Into the parson's orchard did a stealthy figure creep;
  And the silent night was rent with cries, with screams and also
    curse:
  The parson woke and he grabbed his wig, likewise his
    blunderbuss.

8 Then he hurried down the stairs and out into the night;
  In his nightgown and powdered wig he made a funny sight,
  But when he reached the orchard it was he who laughed amain
  For to find the sorry blacksmith caught and held by his own
    chain.

62   Young Johnson

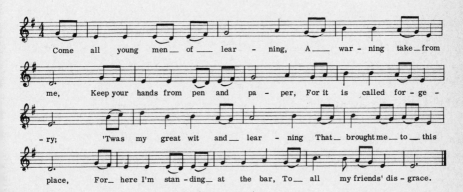

Come all young men of lear - ning, A war - ning take from me, Keep your hands from pen and pa - per, For it is called for - ge - ry; 'Twas my great wit and lear - ning That brought me to this place, For here I'm stan - ding at the bar, To all my friends' dis - grace.

2 His name it was young Johnson,
 So hard his case must be,
No lands nor livings could him save,
 Nor money set him free.
His name it was young Johnson,
 Well drest from top to toe,
To hear himself condemned to die,
 His eyes with tears did flow.

3 The ladies that were standing by,
 Five thousand pounds would give,
To save the life of Johnson,
 If they would him reprieve.
The Jury then stood up and said,
 Ladies that cannot be,
If you'd give ten thousand pounds,
 We cannot set him free.

4 As Johnson rode up Holborn-hill,
 So mildly then spoke he,
I freely forgive all the world,
 And hope they'll forgive me.
Then with a smiling countenance,
 He made a graceful bow,
Farewell my companions all,
 I bid you all adieu.

Holborn-hill: on the way to Tyburn.

'*The day appointed by law for the thief's shame is the day of glory in his own opinion. His procession to Tyburn and his last moments there are all triumphant*': so wrote the novelist, Henry Fielding, in his Enquiry into the Causes of the Late Increase in Robbers (1751). Johnson, *who may or may not have existed in reality, is less of a swashbuckler, more of an elegant gentleman. His crime, forgery, remained a capital offence until early in the nineteenth century. The ballad, like many others dealing with murder and executions, was sung to the carol tune, 'Dives and Lazarus'.*

63   The Highwayman Outwitted

Admiration for the highwayman's daring deeds did not extend to the times when he attempted to rob humble people like the ploughboy or the 'fair damsel'. On those occasions, at least in ballads, it was expected that he would be defeated by the superior wit and resolution of his intended victims.

It's of a rich farmer in Che-shire;___ To the mar-ket his daughter would go, ___ Not thin-king that a-ny would harm her: ___ She'd of-ten been that way be-fore. ___

2 She was met by a rusty [ruffian] highwayman,
  Who caused the young damsel to stand [stay].
  'Your money and clothes now deliver,
  Or else your sweet life is at hand' [you must pay].

3 He stripped this fair damsel stark naked,
  And gave her his bridle to hold;
  And there she stood shivering and shaking,
  Near starved unto death with the cold.

4 She put her left foot in the stirrup,
  And mounted her horse like a man;
  Over hedges and ditches she galloped,
  Crying, 'Catch me, bold rogue, if you can.'

5 The bold rogue he soon followed after,
  Which caused him to puff and to blow.
  Thank God that he never did catch her
  Till she came to her own father's door.

6 'Oh, daughter, dear daughter, what's happened?'
  'Oh, father, to you I will tell;
  I was met by a rusty highwayman.
  Thank God, he has done me no harm.'

7 'Put the grey mare in the stable,
   And spread the white sheet on the floor.'
   She stood there and counted the money,
   She counted five thousand and more.

rusty: ? ruffian.   *like a man*: astride.
starved: cold.

64   Jack Williams the Boatswain

2 I went a-robbing night and day to maintain her both fine and
      gay;
   And what I got I valued it not, but I took it to her straightway.
   At length to Newgate I was sent, bound down in prison
      strong,
   With heavy chains about my legs: she longed to see them on.

3 I sent a letter to my love, some comfort to find;
  Instead of proving kind to me she proved very unkind.
  She in a scornful manner said, 'I'll shun thieves' company.
  So as you have made your bed, down on it you may lie.'

4 I thought these sayings very hard when I'd spent all my store,
  To find she had no more regard for me, now I am low and
      poor.
  All in this lonesome cell I lie, no better I deserve;
  Which makes my blood run cold, when thinking how I'm
      served.

5 I am a boatswain by my trade and a waterman also;
  I maintained her like a lady gay, in fine silks from top to toe,
  But if e'er I gain my liberty a solemn vow I'll make.
  I'll shun all harlots' company for that base strumpet's sake.

6 Now the assizes is over and sentence passed, and hanged I
      must be;
  It grieves my parents to the heart to think on my misery.
  But fortune proved kind to me, that you may plainly see,
  I broke the jail and scaled the wall, and gained my liberty.

*Jack Williams 'went a-robbing night and day' to support a 'lady gay' who
spurned him as soon as he fell foul of the law. Most versions conclude with his
bitter despair as he faces the gallows, but here he miraculously escapes.*

Memento Mori

The Sewing Machine

A young man looks after some stolen property for the woman he is courting.
Despite his unwitting involvement, there are unpleasant consequences.

I'm one of those un - luck - y chaps who once did fall in
love With such a nice, good look - ing girl who seemed just like a
dove; Her hair was black and long, and as cur - ly as e - ver was
seen, And she said she got her live - li - hood by wor - king a sew - ing ma -
- chine. *Chorus* So I fair - ly lost my heart, and I wish I ne - ver had
seen That — dark young girl with her hair in curl who worked at a sew - ing ma - chine.

2 I saw her first near Deansgate at such a dashing shop,
Working Thomas's Number Two – at the window I did stop;
From the signs that passed between us, to Pomona Gardens
    she'd not been,
But she promised to meet if I'd stand treat, when she'd done at
    the sewing machine.

3 I took her to the gardens and for the two I paid,
And as I walked about the grounds, says she, 'I feel afraid
That I shall lose my money', and she gave me such a look,
And said, 'Dear sir, will you take care of this, my
    pocket-book?'

4 I told her not to be afraid, I'd guard it as my life,
And thought how happy I should be if she was my dear wife,
When I heard a cry of 'Stop, thief', and before a word I could
    say
I was collared so tight, and out of my sight my girl had bolted
    away.

5 I asked them what they meant, and I asked them if they knew
Who I was, when they replied, 'I should rather think we do;
For officers are we, and of nailing a watch you're accused,
So beware what you say for against you some day as evidence
   it may be used.'

6 Next morning I was taken up and the officers did tell
The magistrate that they thought to the police I was known
   quite well:
'Though the watch on him could not be found the police
   cannot deceive,
For on him we found a pocket-book containing a
   ticket-of-leave.'

7 The magistrate then shook his head and says, 'Appears quite
   true,
But I'll remand you for a week to see what's known of you.'
Though nothing against me could be found, though
   everywhere they'd been,
Still I got six months in Belle Vue Jail, where I learnt to work a
   machine.

Deansgate: in Manchester.
Thomas's Number Two: type of sewing machine.
Pomona Gardens: where Pomona Dock now is.

ticket-of-leave: document which allowed convict to be released from prison, subject to certain conditions.
work a machine: probably a treadmill.

66   The Slap-bum Tailor

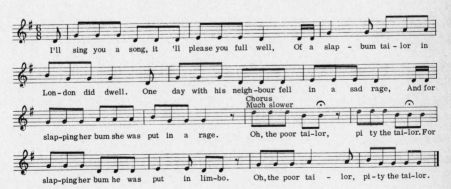

I'll sing you a song, it 'll please you full well, Of a slap - bum tai - lor in Lon - don did dwell. One day with his neigh-bour fell in a sad rage, And for slap-ping her bum she was put in a rage.

Chorus Much slower

Oh, the poor tai-lor, pi - ty the tai-lor. For slap-ping her bum he was put in lim-bo. Oh, the poor tai - lor, pi - ty the tai-lor.

145

2 This woman was a dealer in second-hand clothes;
  One day in the street with a carpet she goes.
  She began for to shake and to toss in the wind:
  'Good lord,' says the tailor, 'Your dust will me blind.'

3 'I value thee not, at my door I will stand,
  For a tailor is but the ninth part of a man.'
  So as he was sewing and taking long stitches
  The dust flew about him and spoiled his new breeches.

4 One day in a passion he called her a whore,
  Then he jumped off his board and he run out of door;
  He fell on his knee, crying, 'Come, madam, come,'
  Then he turned up her clothes and he well slapped her bum.

5 The streets and the lanes was all of an uproar;
  He banged her so hard till her buttocks was sore.
  Some they did laugh and some did cry shame;
  They raised such a mob till the constables came.

6 Then straight to the justice they took him with speed,
  And told how he'd served this poor woman indeed;
  They told he had beat her and slapped her bum,
  When before the justice the tailor did come.

7 'For slapping her bum,' the justice replied,
  'Seven days in the jail the tailor shall lie;
  The poor woman's so ill she can't get out of bed,
  So on bread and water the rogue shall be fed.'

8 So now the poor tailor in limbo do lie;
  He'll remember the carpet when the dust it do fly.
  The lads make their game, crying, 'Run, tailor, run,
  She's a-shaking the carpet, run and slap her bum.'

ninth part of a man: 'Nine tailors make a man,' says the adage (though it is probably a
  corruption of 'Nine tellers make a man': a church bell tolled nine times indicates the
  death of a man).

*Although he apparently has a legitimate grievance against a woman who
insults him and spoils his work, the tailor's rough justice earns him seven days
in limbo (prison).*

146

One is irresistibly reminded here of Hogarth's engravings, 'The Rake's Progress'. Fortunately, this young man realizes in time the error of his ways. Although the ballad has a strong eighteenth-century flavour it was not collected until 1908.

I am a poor lad and my for-tune is bad, And if
e-ver I get rich 'tis a won-der. I've spent all my mo-ney on
girls and strong beer, And what ri-ches I had are all plun-dered.
Field af-ter field___ to mar-ket I sent, Till my land was all
gone and my mo-ney all spent. My heart was so hard that I
ne-ver could re-pent, And 'twas that ___ that brought me to Lim-bo.

2 Once I could run whilst others did lie,
  And strut like a crow in the gutter;
  The people all said that saw me pass by,
  'There goes Mr Fop in a flutter.'
  To the top and top-gallant I hoisted my sails,
  With a fine, fringy cravat and a wig with three tails,
  And now I am ready to gnaw my own nails,
  And drink the cold water of Limbo.

3 I had an old uncle lived down in the west,
  And he heard of my sad disaster.
  Poor soul, after that he could never take no rest,
  For his troubles came faster and faster.
  He come to the gaol to view my sad case,
  And as soon as I saw him I knew his old face;
  I stood gazing on him like one in amaze:
  I wished myself safe out of Limbo.

147

4 'Jack, if I should set you once more on your legs,
   And put you in credit and fashion,
   Oh, will you leave off those old rakish ways,
   And try for to govern your passion?'
   'Yes, Uncle,' says I, 'if you will set me free,
   I surely will always be ruled by thee;
   And I'll labour my bones for the good of my soul,
   And I'll pay them for laying me in Limbo.'

5 He pulled out his purse with three thousand pounds,
   And he counted it out in bright guineas;
   And when I was free from the prison gates
   I went to see Peggy and Jeannie.
   In my old ragged clothes they knew nought of my gold;
   They turned me all out in the wet and the cold.
   You'd a-laughed for to hear how those hussies did scold,
   How they jawed me for laying in Limbo.

6 I'd only been there a very short time
   Before my pockets they then fell to picking;
   I banged them as long as my cane I could hold,
   Until they fell coughing and kicking.
   The one bawled out, 'Murder', the other did scold;
   I banged them as long as my cane I could hold.
   I banged their old bodies for the good of their souls,
   And I paid them for laying in Limbo.

limbo: prison, where the young man of this ballad was confined for debt.

68   The Unfortunate Lad

*Not only lad, but also trooper, soldier, sailor, cowboy, and even maiden: all
these figured as victim in versions of this haunting lament for a victim of
syphilis. The primitive remedies of 'salts and pills of white mercury' were
clearly not very effective.*

As I was a-walk-ing down by the Lock Hos-pi-tal, As I was a-walk-ing one mor-ning of late, Who did I spy but my own dear comrade, Wrapped up in flan-nel, so hard was his fate.

Chorus

Oh, had she but told me when she dis-or-dered me, Had she but told me of it in time, I might have got salts and pills of white mer-cu-ry, Now I'm cut down in the height of my prime.

2 I boldly stepped up to him and kindly did ask him
Why was he wrapped in flannel so white.
'My body is injured and sadly disordered,
All by a young woman, my own heart's delight.

3 'My father oft told me and oftentimes chided me,
Said my wicked way would never do;
But I never minded him, nor ever heeded him,
Always kept up in my own wicked ways.

4 'Get six jolly fellows to carry my coffin,
Six pretty maidens to bear up my pall;
And give to each of them fine bunches of roses,
That they may not smell me as they go along.

5 'Over my coffin put handsful of lavender,
Handsful of lavender on every side;
Bunches of roses all over my coffin,
Saying, "There goes a young man cut down in his prime."

6 'Muffle your drums, play your pipes merrily,
Play the dead march as you go along,
And fire your guns right over my coffin:
There goes an unfortunate lad to his home.'

Lock Hospital: hospital for venereal diseases (from 'lock', female pudendum).
Muffle your drums: evidently the lad is a soldier.

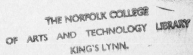
149

VI
Take a Warning from Me:
Cautionary Tales

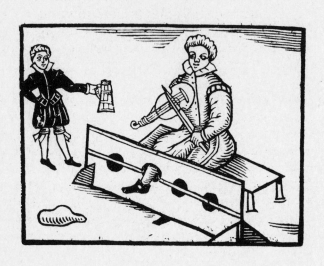

69   ## Prosser's Betting Shop

There's a shop a-round the cor-ner which I vis-it eve-ry day, With my head all full of fi-gures and my po-ckets full of pay; I get out my grea-sy pen-cil and my rag-gy *Ra-cing Blue,* And I try hard to con-vince my-self a kil-ling must be due. I'm

Chorus

do-ing all my mo-ney, do-ing all my mo-ney, Do-ing all my mo-ney at old Pros-ser's bet-ting shop.

2 But before the day is over the bloom has left my cheek;
  The form book lies in ribbons and my cash is up the creek.
  I'm cursing all the jockeys and all the trainers too,
  And the air in Prosser's betting shop turns several shades of
      blue.

3 Oh, I've tried the Level Method and the Graded Staking Plan,
  And I've used up every system that is known to racing man;
  But for all my fond researches amongst the sporting prose,
  When it comes to picking winners, well, I couldn't pick my
      nose.

4 Now when my punting's over and I'm laid out on cold stones
  That bookie'll walk the column to identify my bones.
  Here's one last tip for Prosser, it's a racing certainty:
  Wherever my body's lying it won't be in the first three.

*The writer of this ballad, Dennis O'Neill, dedicates it 'to all the gambling
wasters and industrious small bookmakers of Wales, and in particular to the
citizens of Merthyr Tudful' (Tydfil). He asserts that the town has a greater
number of betting shops per head than any other in the United Kingdom. The
tune is 'Wait for the Waggon', otherwise known as 'The Putter'.*

70   Off to Epsom Races

When I was young and in my prime, a-bout twen-ty-four years
old, I spent my time in va-ni-ty, a-long with the la-dies so
bold, A-long with the la-dies so bold.
Var.(a)
v.3 I hired a coach and six bay hors-es and

2 With my silver buckles all round my wrists and a cane all in
    my hand,
  All over the nation I do go like a farmer's son so grand.

3 I hired a coach and six bay horses and servants to wait on me,
  For I did intend my money to spend, and that you can plainly
    see.

4 I steered my coach to Epsom races all on one Derby Day,
  And there I did spend ten thousand pounds all in the delight of
    one day.

5 I steered my coach back home again; the crops they did run
    small,
  For I was a broken-down gentleman, and that was the worst
    of all.

6 The landlord came all for his rent, and bailiffs he brought
    three;
  They took away all I had got and they swore that they would
    have me.

7 My wife at home she does lament, and children round her cry,
  While I all in some prison do lay until the day that I die.

'The Broken-down Gentleman' is an alternative title for this sad story of ruin by gambling and high living. It has an eighteenth-century ring, was popular in the nineteenth, and survived in oral tradition until the twentieth.

71   All for the Grog

One of the evil consequences of drinking – shortage of money – is here treated with altogether too much gusto to act as an entirely convincing deterrent. The song was widely known among sailors (with 'the Western Ocean' in the chorus), though here it comes from a country singer. It was the custom at one time for the singer progressively to remove his clothes as he proceeded through the song.

My old hat that I got on, the crownd of him is gone, And the rim's all gone to a sut-ter. If I on-ly had one more, if I on-ly had a score, I would keep my old hat in re-mem-brance. Here's all for the grog, the bon-ny, bon-ny grog, Here's all for the beer and to-bac-co. I've spent all my bloom-ing tin with the las-sies drinking gin, And a-cross the bri-ny o-cean I must wan-der.

2 My old coat that I got on,
   The sleeves of 'im are gone,
   And the tail's all gone to a sutter.
   If I only had one more,
   If I only had a score,
   I would keep my jacket in remembrance.

3 My old weskit I got on,
   The front of 'im is gone,
   And the back's all gone, *etc*.

4 My old shirt that I got on,
   The tail of 'im is gone,
   And the front's all gone, *etc*.

5 My old shoes that I got on,
   The soles o' them are gone,
   And the tops all gone, *etc*.

6 My old socks that I got on,
   The feet o' them are gone,
   And the tops all gone, *etc*.

gone to a sutter: has become worn out.

153

72   Such a Nobby Head of Hair

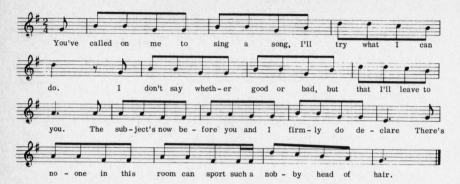

You've called on me to sing a song, I'll try what I can do. I don't say wheth-er good or bad, but that I'll leave to you. The sub-ject's now be-fore you and I firm-ly do de-clare There's no-one in this room can sport such a nob-by head of hair.

2 I go to all places of amusement and see everything that's new —
  Balls, plays, White Conduit Gardens and the Eagle Tavern,
    too;
  I feel prouder than Prince Albert when the ladies see me there,
  To hear the buzz of admiration at my nobby head of hair.

3 Although my hair is elegant it often gets me into scrapes —
  At the Zoological the other day 'twas well pulled by the apes —
  And in making my escape from them I was grappled by a bear;
  It fancied that I was its cub by my nobby head of hair.

4 Not liking this brute treatment from the gardens I did roam —
  I caught a lady ogling me — I asked to see her home.
  Her husband we met on the road, he asunder us did tear,
  Then he dragged me through a horse-pond by my nobby head
    of hair.

5 He left me near dead with affright and wet through to the skin;
  A mob soon came around me, they did nought but leer and
    grin.
  A policeman took me into custody and solemnly did swear
  I a member of the swell mob was, by my nobby head of hair.

6 To the magistrate my innocence I pleaded, but in vain;
  He said, 'To prison you must go, your guilt it is quite plain.'
  So to the treadmill I was sent, put on the silent system there,
  But what grieved me most they cut off all my nobby head of
    hair.

7 I thought it would have drove me mad but it grew again so
    fast,
  It put me in such spirits that I soon forgot the past.
  The mill it dragged down all my fat – I looked so lean and
    spare,
  My friends they knew me only by my nobby head of hair.

8 But now that I am free again I'm happy as a king;
  That's one reason why tonight, you see, I've come here to
    sing.
  But this is a thing you can't deny, it is a thing most rare,
  To see a handsome chap like me with such a nobby head of
    hair.

Nobby: very smart; the word is still occasionally used.
White Conduit Gardens: pleasure grounds on an eminence above the tunnel connecting
  Regent's and Paddington Canals.
Eagle Tavern: music hall, mentioned in 'Pop Goes the Weasel'.
swell mob: criminal fraternity.

*The singer's vanity leads him into trouble, but all ends happily. The reference
to Prince Albert dates the ballad between 1840 and 1861.*

73   Jock Hawk's Adventures in Glasgow

*The countryman and the sailor, alike unused to the ways of the city, were easy
meat for sharpers and prostitutes. The song was known all over Scotland 'in
farm kitchens and feeing markets' towards the end of the nineteenth century.*

One night I in to Glas-ga went To spend my pen-ny
fee;_____ 'Twas then a girl___ gave con-sent To bear me com-pa-
Chorus
-ny. Tum a high tum a do, tum a high tum
day, Tum a high tum a do, tum a high tum day.___

2 I said I was a stranger,
   And Glasga did not know;
   She said there was no danger
   If I wi' her would go.

3 She linked her arm into mine,
   And we walked down the street;
   And I never dreaded any harm,
   Though hundreds we did meet.

4 But as we did pass through a crowd
   I heard a whisper say:
   'D'ye see Jock Hawk? He's got a miss,
   But he'll repent that play.'

5 We walked down Jamaica Street
   And through the Broomielaw,
   Where organ lads played rich and sweet,
   And fiddlers ane or twa.

6 We then into a tavern went,
   Where I called for some gin;
   And the lads and lassies a' looked up
   And laughed as we came in.

7 I scarce had got the gin poured out
   When in came half a score
   O' sailor lads and girls so nice
   I never saw before.

8 I handed each a glass o' gin,
   And they drank it up richt free;
   And ilka ane aye drank success
   To my bonnie young lass and me.

9 The spree kept up wi' mirth and song
   Till it was growin' clear,
   And then a knock cam' to the door:
   'All hands on deck appear.'

10 Some o' them snatched a parting kiss,
And other said 'Goodbye';
And the hindmost ane as he passed out
Said, 'Jock, ye've a' to pey.'

11 They've ta'en frae me my watch and chain,
My spleuchan and my knife;
I wonder that they did not tak'
My little spunk o' life.

12 They've stripped me o' my braw new coat,
My waistcoat and my shune;
And for my hat, I never saw't
Since first I called the gin.

13 Now home frae Glasga I'd to gae
Baith naked and quite bare,
And back again I widna gang
To get a spree nae mair.

fee: money paid at hiring fair to seal engagement.

spleuchan: tobacco pouch.
spunk: spark.

74   Maggie May

After his voyage the sailor goes on the town with his earnings, and is robbed by a good-time girl: the classic story, in the form of Maggie May, is something of a local anthem in Liverpool, though versions are known much further afield.

Come ga-ther round, you sai-lor lads, and lis-ten to my plea, And when you've heard my tale you'll pi-ty me. I was a bloo-dy fool in the port of Li-ver-pool, The first time that I came home from sea. We was paid off at the Home from the port of Sier-ra Leone, And three pound ten a week it was my pay. With a po-cket full of tin I was ve-ry soon ta-ken in By a girl with the name of Maggie May. Oh, Maggie, Maggie May, they have taken her a-way To walk up-on Van Diemen's cru-el shore. She robbed so ma-ny sai-lors and dosed so ma-ny wha-lers, And she'll ne-ver roam down Lime Street a-ny more.

2 Too well I do remember when I first met Maggie May,
She was cruising up and down old Canning Place,
With a figure so divine like a frigate of the line,
And me, being a sailor, I gave chase.
Next morning I awoke, I was flat and stony broke,
No jacket, trousers, waistcoat could I find.
When I asked her where they were, she said to me, 'Kind sir,
They're down in Kelly's pawnshop, number nine.'

3 To the pawnshop I did go but no clothes there could I find,
And a policeman came and took that girl away.
The judge he guilty found her for robbing a homeward-
   bounder,
And he paid her passage back to Botany Bay.
Oh, Maggie, *etc.*

the Home: the Sailors' Home in   *tin*: money.
  Liverpool.   *Van Diemen's Land*: Tasmania.

Ratcliffe Highway

'A reservoir of dirt, drunkenness and drabs': such was Mayhew's description in the 1850s of Ratcliffe Highway (the line of which, near to and parallel with the present Cable Street, has long since been built over). In the ballad an intended victim spiritedly turns the tables on a sailortown 'damsel'.

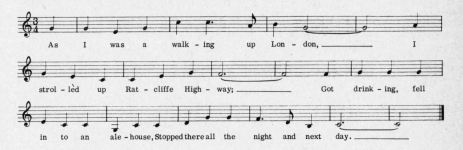

As I was a walk-ing up Lon-don, _____ I strol-lèd up Rat-cliffe High-way; _____ Got drink-ing, fell in to an ale-house, Stopped there all the night and next day. _____

2 With a buxom young lass set beside me,
   Asked me if I'd money to sport;
   I called for a bottle of wine, changed a guinea,
   She says, 'My brave boy, that's the sort.'

3 The bottles were brought on the tables,
   And glasses for everyone;
   I asked for the change of my guinea:
   She tipped me the verse of a song.

4 The young damsel she flew in a passion,
   She placed her two hands on her hips,
   Saying, 'Young man, you don't know the fashion:
   You think you're on board of your ship.'

5 Now I said, 'Miss, if this be your fashion,
   Your fashion I will not abide;
   So if you don't give me the change of my guinea,
   I'll give you a dingie or broadside.'

6 Now the bottles that stood on the table,
   So brisk and so nimble they flew;
   This young damsel she flew on the floor,
   Shruck, 'Murder, oh, what shall I do?'

7 The gold watch that laid on the mantel,
  The change of my guinea I see;
  I put it into my pocket,
  Unto the door I flew.

8 Now the night it was dark in my favour,
  To the water I gently did creep;
  Got into a boat bound for Devon,
  Got safely on board of my ship.

9 Come all you buxom young fellows,
  A warning take by me:
  If you would go strolling up London,
  Just mind what money you pay.

10 For the girls they are sure to entice you,
   Your mind they will quickly disrange;
   If by chance you should tip them a guinea
   You may go to hell for your change.

76 Down by the Dark Arches

Like Jock Hawk in Glasgow (no. 73), the unwary man abroad in London is robbed of everything, even his clothes. To fill the cup of misery the woman decoy for the thieves is a ballad singer. Appropriately, the song itself appeared on a street ballad, with the tune of 'The Green Bushes' indicated (though that is not used here). Instead of 'under the railway' the dark arches were 'near the Adelphi' (a well-known terrace just east of Charing Cross).

As I walked out one day in July A fair pret-ty dam-sel there
I did es - py, Sing-ing 'Vil-li-kins and Di - nah', so
sweet and so gay. Down by the dark ar-ches un - der the rail-way, Oh,
yes, she did, so she did, whack fol the rid-dle ol day.

2 I stepped up to her so gay and so free,
  And for the same ballad I paid one ha'penny.
  'Will you be my sweetheart?' to her I did say,
  Down by *etc.*
  Oh, yes I did, so I did, *etc.*

3 'Oh, no, my dear chap, that never can be.
  There's a man there in blue and he's watching for me;
  And if he should see me, what would he say?'
  Down by *etc.*
  Oh, yes she did, *etc.*

4 At last she consented, away we both went.
  Five shillings on oysters and lobsters I spent,
  And six drops of brandy for her I did pay.
  Down by *etc.*
  Oh, yes I did, *etc.*

5 Then up came a chap with a black eye and a stick;
  He drank up my brandy and broke my pickwick.
  'Pop goes the weasel' to me he did say,
  Down by, *etc.*
  Oh, yes he did, so he did, *etc.*

6 He squared up to me and pulled my watch out,
  He spoilt my beaver and damaged my snout.
  He kicked me in the gutter and there I did lay,
  Down by, *etc.*
  Oh, yes he did, *etc.*

7 I lay in the gutter till four in the morn,
  As naked as any poor creature was born;
  And when I awakened so stiff there I lay,
  Down by, *etc.*
  Oh, yes I did, *etc.*

8 Four bobbies came up and, to my surprise,
  I'd got no shirt on to cover my thighs.
  They put me on a stretcher and bore me away
  From beneath the dark arches, *etc.*
  Oh, yes they did, so they did, *etc.*

9 I sent to me mother for money and clothes,
Likewise a doctor to patch up my nose.
'You've not had fair play,' to me he did say,
Down under, *etc.*
Oh, yes he did, *etc.*

10 Now all you young chaps take warning by me,
And never go courting when you're out on the spree;
Never take those young ladies from out of their way,
Down to the dark arches, *etc.*
Oh, yes I did, *etc.*

oysters and lobsters: considered to have aphrodisiac properties.
pickwick: cigar.
beaver: hat.

77   **The Bold Cockney**

The countryman is often worsted when he goes to town, but sometimes the balance is redressed. When the townsman attempts to assert his dominance in the country, he is liable to come off second best.

A story of a Cockney I will now relate, That
went to the country to seek for a mate; And put in his pocket two
hand-fuls of gold, With a sword by his side to
make him look bold. With a sword by his side to make him look bold.

2 He rode till he came into fair Huntingdon,
And there did dismount at the sign of the Crown;
For a beautiful damsel appeared in his sight,
Which made him resolve there to tarry for the night.

162

3 He said, 'Pretty damsel, if you will be mine,
   My gold and my silver and all shall be thine';
   But she said, 'Sir, your passion must now be assuaged,
   For I to a ploughboy am lately engaged.'

4 The ploughboy being near did hear him speak so,
   And said to the Cockney, 'I know what I know,
   For this is the damsel that is to be mine,
   But if you can gain her she then shall be thine.'

5 'You impudent fellow, what makes you to prate?
   For I with my weapon will soon break your pate.
   You're nought but a bumpkin come from the ploughtail,
   And can handle nought but a whip or a flail.'

6 'Oh, then,' says the ploughboy, 'let's go to that field;
   Before we give over one of us must yield.
   Let it never be reckoned or by any said
   That a ploughboy's afraid to fight for his maid.'

7 They fought half an hour as I've heard them say
   Before it was known which would gain the day;
   Till at last the brave ploughboy gave Cockney a fall,
   And said, 'Mister Cockney, you shall pay for all.'

8 'My gold and my silver and all that I have
   I freely will give you my life now to save;
   Let this ne'er be said with a strange country lie,
   But take me to London and there let me die.'

9 His gold and his silver and all that he had
   The ploughboy received and gave to his maid;
   Let it ne'er then be reckoned nor by any said
   That a ploughboy's afraid to fight for his maid.

Rosemary Lane was a thoroughfare near London Docks renowned for its street stalls. (It is now called Royal Mint Street.) This version comes from a Staffordshire chainmaker, Lucy Woodall, who remembered the women singing it at work in the chainshop.

2 One day a young sailor
  Came to our house to tea;
  And this was the commencement
  Of my misery.

3 When supper was over
  He hung down his head,
  Then he asked for a candle
  To light him to bed.

4 I gave him a candle
  As a maiden should do;
  Then he vowed and declared
  That I should go too.

5 Me like a silly girl
  Was thinking no harm,
  So I jumped into bed with him
  To keep myself warm.

6 Early next morning
  When the young sailor rose
  He threw in my apron
  Two handfuls of gold.

7 'Oh, take it, oh, take it,
   For the wrong I have done;
   I have left you a daughter
   Or else a fine son.'

8 'If it be a daughter
   She shall wait upon me,
   But if it's a sonny,
   He shall cross the blue sea.

9 'He shall wear a blue jacket
   And his cap lined with gold;
   He shall cross the blue ocean
   Like his young father bold.'

10 Now all you young lasses
   Take a warning from me:
   Never trust a young sailor
   Whoe'er he may be.

11 They kiss you, they court you,
   They swear they'll be true,
   But the very next moment
   They'll bid you adieu.

12 Like the flower in the garden
   When its beauty's all done,
   So you see what I've come to
   Through loving that one.

13 No father, no mother,
   No friend in the world,
   So me and my baby
   To the workhouse must go.

The Fair Maid of Islington

The moral here is perhaps somewhat immoral: if you sell your favours, make sure you obtain the agreed price. The ballad dates from the late seventeenth century. It was reprinted in the nineteenth, and recorded to a different tune in the twentieth (A Merry Progress to London, Argo ZFB60, 1967). The two tunes originally indicated were 'Sellenger's Round' and 'Caper and Ferk It'. The latter (better known as 'Under the Greenwood Tree', but having no connection with Thomas Hardy) has been used here.

There was a fair maid at *Is - ling - ton* as I heard ma - ny tell; And she would to fair *Lon - don* go, fine Apples and Pears to sell: And as she pass'd a - long the street, with her bas - ket on — her arm, There did — she with a Vint - ner meet, this fair Maid thought no harm.

2 'Good-morrow, fair Maid,' the Vintner said;
   'what have you got here to sell?'
'Fine Apples and Pears, kind Sir,' she said,
   'if you please to taste them, well.'
He tasted of this fair Maid's Fruit,
   and he lik'd it wondrous well;
And then he crav'd of this fair Maid,
   how many a Penny she'd sell.

3 'Sir, here you shall have six,' she said,
   'and here you shall have ten;
I sold no more, but just before,
   to some Inns of Court Gentlemen.'
Now while he by the Dam'sel staid,
   her Body he did eye,
At length he crav'd of this fair Maid,
   one Night with him to lie:

4 'Thy Beauty doth so please my Eye,
   and dazels so my sight,

That now of all my Liberty,
   I am deprived quite:
And therefore, Love, be kind to me,
   and let us toy and play,
It is but one small Courtesie,
   then do not say me Nay.'

5 'Sir, if you lye with me one Night,
   as you propound to me,
I do expect that you should prove
   Both courteous, kind, and free:
And for to tell you all in short,
   it will cost you five Pound.'
'A Match, a Match,' the Vintner said,
   and so let this go round.

6 When he had lain with her all Night,
   her Money she did crave:
'O stay,' quoth he, 'the other Night,
   and thy Money thou shalt have.'
'I cannot stay, nor I will not stay,
   I needs must now be gone,'
'Why then thou maist thy Money go look,
   for Money I'll pay thee none.'

7 This Maid she made no more ado,
   but to [a] Justice went,
And unto him she made her Moan,
   who did her Case lament:
She said she [ha]d a Cellar Let out,
   To a Vintner in the Town,
And how that he did then agree
   five Pound to pay her down.

8 'But now,' quoth she, 'the Case is thus,
   no Rent that he will pay;
Therefore, your Worship, I beseech,
   to send for him this Day.'
Then strait the Justice for him sent,
   and asked the Reason why,

That he would pay this Maid no Rent?
   To which he did reply,

9 'Although I hired a Cellar of her,
   and the Possession was mine,
I ne'r put any thing into it,
   but one poor Pipe of Wine;
Therefore my Bargain it was hard,
   as you may plainly see,
I from my Freedom was debar'd;
   then, good Sir, favour me.'

10 This fair Maid being ripe of Wit,
   she strait reply'd agen;
'There was two Butts [more] lay at the Door,
   why did you not roul them in?
You had your Freedom and your Will,
   as is to you well known;
Therefore I do desire still
   for to receive my own.'

11 The Justice hearing of their Case,
   did there give Order straight,
That he the Money should pay down,
   she should no longer wait:
Withal he told the Vintner plain,
   if he a Tennant be;
He must expect to pay the same,
   for he could not sit Rent-free.

12 But when her Money she had got,
   she put it into her Purse,
And clapt her Hand o' the Cellar-door,
   and said it was never the worse:
Which caused the People all to Laugh,
   to see this Vintner fine,
Out-witted by a Country Girl
   about his Pipe of Wine.

80   Little Ball of Yarn

One wonders whether overtly moral songs like this do not do more to make young men think of seduction than to make young women think of the dangers.

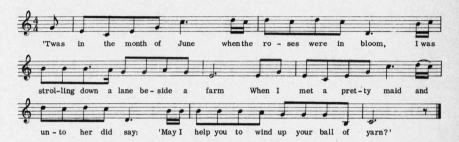

'Twas in the month of June when the ro - ses were in bloom, I was strol-ling down a lane be-side a farm When I met a pret-ty maid and un - to her did say: 'May I help you to wind up your ball of yarn?'

2 Now we walked and talked a lot and loving soon we got;
   Soon we were talking all of love.
   She said, 'Oh, pardon me, you're a stranger I can see,
   But you cannot help to wind up my ball of yarn.'

3 After nine months passed away, oh, I met that maid one day
   With a bonny boy a-bouncing on her arm.
   I said, 'Oh, pardon me, miss, did you ever think of this
   While a-winding up your little ball of yarn?'

4 Now all you young and old, take a warning when you're told,
   Do not rise too early in the morn;
   Like the blackbird and the thrush, keep one hand upon your
      bush,
   And the other on your little ball o' yarn.

81   The Ledbury Parson

The Reverend John Jackson, Rector of Ledbury in Herefordshire from 1860 until 1891, was suspended from duty for two years (1869–71) while an investigation was held into a complaint that he was the father of one of his servants' children. He was exonerated and restored, but the poor man's alleged misdeeds were magnified in a ballad which continued to reverberate in the neighbourhood for over a hundred years.

In Ledbury town in Herefordshire They rucked up a row with the
parson there. This pious gentleman, so they say, Was
far too fond of going astray. So if going astray should
be your plan Just think of the Ledbury clergyman.

2 This pious gentleman did, you know,
  A very religious example show:
  'Stead o' learning the folk to preach and pray
  He was kissing and cuddling night and day.

3 This parson he was a roving blade,
  He courted the cook and the servant maid;
  Gave out his text and winked his eye:
  'Come, kiss me girls and multiply.'

4 Now sooner or later the tale went round
  That a young chickabiddy had come to town,
  And its features did the truth disclose
  Of the Ledbury parson's eyes and nose.

5 They summoned him up and made him pay
  One half a crown a week, they say.
  So clergymen, my warning take,
  And think of the Ledbury parson's fate.

6 This parson got in a terrible rage,
  He swore to the child he never would pay;
  And to cure his sins he preached and prayed
  With Lizzie the cook and Kitty the maid.

7 Then up to the church then toddled the cook,
  And in her arms this child she took;
  And the parson on them glanced his eye:
  'Oh, look, it's your daddy,' the cook did cry.

8 Now this parson said 'twas his desire,
    And from the sinful world retire;
    And join the mormons he would strive,
    And marry one hundred and fifty wives.

9 Then from the church he got the sack:
    They took the surplice off his back,
    And they wouldn't allow him to preach and pray
    Till ten long years had passed away.

10 Now, married men, just mind your eye:
    Don't get kissing and cuddling on the sly.
    Those single chaps might go astray,
    But they better get married without delay.

82   Poison in a Glass of Wine

*'Beware of jealousy': the message here is quite simple, though one should
perhaps add the advice that it is inadvisable to administer glasses of poisoned
wine. The ballad was widely known, under a variety of titles: 'Oxford City',
'Newport Street' and 'Down in the Groves'.*

A fair young maid went out to ser-vice; Her mis-tress in-vi-ted young
men to tea. She had-n't been gone one sin-gle hour
Be - fore her own young man came in.

2 He caught her dancing with another;
    A jealous thought crept through his mind
    Of how to destroy his own true lover:
    He poured some poison in a glass of wine.

171

3 So soon she drank, so soon she uttered:
   'Oh, pray, young man, come take me home;
   For that glass of wine that you have given me
   Will surely carry me to my grave.'

4 'If that will carry you to your grave, love,
   Then I will drink of the same, you see;
   And hand in hand we'll die together:
   Young lovers beware of jealousy.

5 'Too young to court, too young to marry,
   Too young to think of the wedding day;
   For when you're married you're bound for ever:
   Young lovers beware of jealousy.'

83 There Was a Lady All Skin and Bone

The theme of an elegant lady confronted by grim death was widespread in the Middle Ages, in sermon, story, iconography and balladry. This nursery rhyme may well date back to those times, though its first printed version appeared in about 1783, in Gammer Gurton's Garland. The text concludes with a sort of stage direction: 'Here the lady screams'.

There was a la - dy__ all__ skin and bone, And__ such a
la - dy was ne - ver__ known. It __ hap-pened on a __ ho - ly
day This__ la - dy__ went __ to _____ church to pray.

2 And when she came unto the stile
   She tarried there a little while;
   And when she came unto the door
   She tarried there a little more.

172

3 But when she came into the aisle
   She had a sad and woeful smile;
   She'd come a long and weary mile
   Her sin and sorrow to beguile.

4 And she walked up and she walked down,
   And she saw a dead man upon the ground;
   And from his nose unto his chin
   The worms crept out and the worms crept in.

5 Then the lady to the sexton said:
   'Shall I be so when I am dead?'
   And the sexton to the lady said:
   'You'll be the same when you are dead.'

VII

My Heart to You:
True Love and False

84   The Magpie Said, 'Come In'

Family opposition was (and is) often a formidable obstacle to the course of true love. Here, the subject is treated as (literally) knock-about farce.

I lingered near a cottage door, and the magpie said:'Come in, come in,' The magpie said: 'Come in.' The door was open and I went in, and I saw standing there A maiden with a dimpled chin, a-combing her back hair, back hair, A-combing her back hair.

* The shorter verses start here.

2 A light surprise was in her eyes,
 And still she did not frown;
 But even smiled, this pretty child,
 And the magpie said, 'Sit down, sit down,'
 And the magpie said, 'Sit down.'

3 I sat down in her father's chair,
 And the magpie said, 'Kiss her, kiss her,'
 And the magpie said, 'Kiss her.'
 And yet the maiden did not speak,
 Which made me think: I will;
 And as the red rushed to her cheek,
 She looked more lovely still, still, still,
 She looked more lovely still.

4 But when in haste I grasped her waist,
 She screamed out, 'Oh dear, no.'
 It was so nice I kissed her twice,
 And the magpie said, 'Bravo, bravo,'
 And the magpie said, 'Bravo.'

5 I heard some footsteps stumbling in,
 And the magpie said, 'Get out, get out,'
 And the magpie said, 'Get out.'
 Her father's voice was like a rasp,
 And swearing he began;
 And I experienced the grasp,
 The grasp of an honest man, man, man,
 The grasp of an honest man.

6 He rained such blows upon my clothes,
 I feel them to this day;
 He kicked me, too, as out I flew,
 And the magpie said, 'Hooray, hooray.'
 And the magpie said, 'Hooray.'

7 I was going down the garden path,
 And the magpie said, 'Look out, look out,'
 And the magpie said, 'Look out.'
 It was too late, her brother, Fred,

Gave me one on my nose;
He laid me in the onion bed
In all my Sunday clothes, clothes, clothes,
In all my Sunday clothes.

8 He ran me down the garden path;
Immediately I fell.
He put me in the water trough,
And the magpie said, 'Farewell, farewell,'
And the magpie said, 'Farewell.'

9 Across the fields he chased me, too,
He nearly made me fly;
And the magpie chattered and he laughed,
And shouted out, 'Goodbye, goodbye.'
And the magpie said, 'Goodbye.'

85 Amang the Blue Flowers and the Yellow

*Child (his no. 25) calls this 'Willie's Lyke-Wake', remarking that 'The
device of a lover's feigning death as a means of winning a shy mistress enjoys a
considerable popularity in European ballads.' This version telescopes the story
by omitting (after verse 2) the advice to sham death given in analogues. One
cannot help feeling that the whole thing is not cricket, though Child's Euro-
peans would no doubt not agree.*

2 'O, is she an heiress or lady fine,
    As the sun shines over the valley,
    That she winna tak nae pity on thee,
    Amang the blue flowers an' the yellow?'

3 'Though a' your kin were aboot yon bower,
    As the sun shines over the valley,
    Ye shall not be a maiden one single hour,
    Amang the blue flowers an' the yellow.

4 'For maid ye cam here without a convoy,
    As the sun shines over the valley,
    And ye shall return wi' a horse and a boy,
    Amang the blue flowers an' the yellow.

5 'Ye cam here a maiden sae meek and mild,
    As the sun shines over the valley,
    But ye shall gae hame a wedded wife wi' a child,
    Amang the blue flowers an' the yellow.'

86   The Banks of Sweet Dundee

Villainy and virtue, blood and tears, innocence triumphant: here are the ingredients of a strong nineteenth-century melodrama. The ballad has remained popular with country singers until recent years.

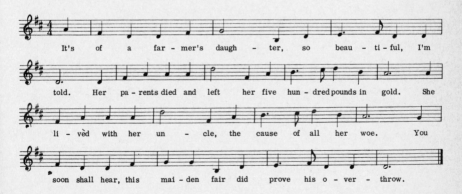

It's of a far-mer's daugh-ter, so beau-ti-ful, I'm told. Her pa-rents died and left her five hun-dred pounds in gold. She li-vèd with her un-cle, the cause of all her woe. You soon shall hear, this mai-den fair did prove his o-ver-throw.

177

2 Her uncle had a ploughboy, young Mary loved him well,
And in her uncle's garden their tales of love would tell;
But there was a wealthy squire who oft came her to see,
But still she loved her ploughboy on the Banks of sweet
    Dundee.

3 It was one summer's morning, her uncle went straightway,
He knocked at her bedroom door and unto her did say:
'Come rise up, pretty maiden, a lady you may be:
The squire is waiting for you on the Banks of sweet Dundee.'

4 'A fig for all your squires, your lords and dukes likewise;
My William appears to me like diamonds in my eyes.'
'Begone, unruly female, you ne'er shall happy be;
For I mean to banish William from the Banks of sweet
    Dundee.'

5 The press-gang came to William when he was all alone;
He boldly fought for liberty, but they were six to one.
The blood did flow in torrents, – 'Pray kill me now,' said he,
'I would rather die for Mary on the Banks of sweet Dundee.'

6 This maid one day was walking, lamenting for her love;
She met the wealthy squire down in her uncle's grove.
He put his arms around her. 'Stand off, base man,' said she;
'You sent the only lad I love from the Banks of sweet
    Dundee.'

7 He clasped his arms around her and tried to throw her down,
Two pistols and a sword she spied beneath his morning
    gown.
Young Mary took the pistols, the sword he used so free,
But she did fire and shot the squire on the Banks of sweet
    Dundee.

8 Her uncle overheard the noise and hastened to the ground:
'O, since you've killed the squire I'll give you your death
    wound.'
'Stand off, then,' said young Mary, 'undaunted I will be';
She trigger drew, her uncle slew, on the Banks of sweet
    Dundee.

9 A doctor soon was sent for, a man of noted skill,
   Likewise came his daughter, for him to sign his will.
   He willed his gold to Mary who fought so manfully,
   And closed his eyes, no more to rise, on the Banks of sweet
        Dundee.

his daughter: the uncle's.

87 Blackberry Fold

In 'The Banks of Sweet Dundee' (no. 86) a rascally squire who attempts to force a maiden is killed by her with his own weapon. Here, another offender in similar circumstances is merely wounded. The girl's spirit so impresses him that he recovers and marries her, or, as the original ballad sheet has it, 'he made her his lady instead of his w----'.

It's _ of a rich squi-re in _ Bris-tol doth dwell. There are la - dies of ho - nour that _ love _ him well, But _ all was in vain, _ in _ vain, it is said, For _ he was in love with a charm-ing milk - maid.

2 As the squire and his sister did sit in the hall,
   And as they were talking to one and to all;
   And as they were singing each other a song,
   Pretty Betsy the milkmaid came tripping along.

3 'Do you want any new milk?' pretty Betsy did say.
   'Oh, yes,' said the squire, 'step in pretty maid.
   It is your fair body that I do adore.
   Was there ever a lover so wounded before?'

4 'Oh, hold your tongue, squire, and let me go free;
   Do not make your game on my poverty.
   There are ladies of honour more fitter for you
   Than I, the poor milkmaid, brought up from the cows.'

179

5 A ring from his finger he instantly drew,
  And right in the middle he broke it in two;
  And half he gave to her as I have been told,
  And they both went a-walking to Blackberry Fold.

6 'O Betsy, O Betsy, let me have my will,
  So constant a squire I'll prove to you still;
  And if you deny me in this open field,
  Why, the first time I'll force you and make you yield.'

7 With hugging and struggling poor Betsy got free,
  And with her [his?] own weapon she ran him quite through.
  Then home to her master like lightning she flew,
  Saying, 'Oh, my dear master,' with tears in her eyes,
  'I've wounded the squire and I'm afraid dead he lies.'

8 The coach was got ready, the squire was brought home;
  The doctor was sent for to heal up the wound.
  Pretty Betsy was sent for, the gay maiden fair,
  Which wounded the squire, drove his heart in a snare.

9 The parson was sent for this couple to wed,
  And she did enjoy the sweet marriage bed.
  It's better be honest if ever so poor,
  For he made her his lady instead of his whore.

88   Lord Bateman

Bateman, travelling in Turkey, is imprisoned, but later freed by Sophia, the daughter of his captor. She and Bateman, having fallen in love, vow to marry no one else for seven years. After a period of seven years and fourteen days (the delay is not explained) she travels to England and finds that Bateman is about to marry. She presents herself; he duly renounces his bride and marries Sophia. The tale was told in Germany, Scandinavia, Italy and Spain. The English ballad (first licensed in 1624) may have been influenced by the story (dating from about 1300) that Gilbert à Becket, father of Thomas, was captured while on a crusade and freed by a Saracen woman who later travelled to England to marry him.

Lord Bateman was a noble lord, A noble lord of high degree. He put his foot upon ship-board, Some foreign country he would go see.

2 He sailed east and sailed west,
  Until he came to fair Turkey,
Where he was taken and put in prison,
  Until his life was quite weary.

3 And in this prison there grew a tree,
  It grew so stout and it grew so strong,
Where he was chained by his middle,
  Until his life was almost gone.

4 The Turk he had an only daughter,
  The fairest creature ever my eyes did see,
She stole the keys of her father's prison,
  And swore Lord Bateman she would set free!

5 'Have you got houses, have you got lands
  Or does Northumberland belong to thee?
What would you give to the fair young lady,
  That out of prison would set you free?'

6 'I have got houses, I have got lands,
  And half Northumberland belongs to me,
I'll give it all to the fair young lady,
  That out of prison would set me free.'

7 O then she took him to her father's palace,
  And gave to him the best of wine,
And every health she drank unto him,
  'I wish Lord Bateman that you were mine.'

8 Now for seven long years I'll make a vow,
  For seven long years and keep it strong,
If you will wed no other woman,
  That I will wed no other man.'

181

9 O then she took me to her father's harbour,
      And gave to me a ship of fame,
   'Farewell, farewell, my dear Lord Bateman,
      I'm afraid I shall never see you again.'

10 Now seven long years were gone and past,
      And fourteen long days well known to me,
   She packed up her gay clothing,
      And Lord Bateman she would go see.

11 And when she came to Lord Bateman's castle,
      So boldly now she rang the bell,
   'Who's there?' cried the young porter,
      'Who's there? – now come unto me tell.'

12 'O is this Lord Bateman's castle,
      Or is his Lordship here within?'
   'O yes, O yes,' cried the proud young porter,
      'He's just taking his young bride in.'

13 'Oh then tell him to send me a slice of bread
      And a bottle of the best wine,
   And not forgetting the fair young lady,
      That did release him when close confined.'

14 Away away went that proud young porter,
      Away away and away went he,
   Until he came to Lord Bateman's door,
      Down on his bended knees fell he.

15 'What news, what news, my young porter,
      What news have you brought unto me?'
   'There is the fairest of all young ladies,
      That ever my two eyes did see.

16 'She has got rings on every finger,
      And round one of them she has got three,
   And such gay gold hanging round her middle
      As would buy Northumberland for thee.

17 'She tells you to send her a slice of bread,
    And a bottle of the best wine,
And not forgetting the fair young lady,
    That did release you when close confined.'

18 Lord Bateman then in a passion flew,
    And broke his sword in splinters three,
Saying, 'I will give all my father's riches.
    If that Sophia has crossed the sea.'

19 Then up spoke this young bride's mother,
    Who never was heard to speak so free,
'You'll not forget my only daughter,
    If Sophia has crossed the sea.'

20 'I own I made a bride of your daughter,
    She's neither the better nor worse for me,
She came to me with her horse and saddle,
    She may go home in her coach and three.'

21 Lord Bateman prepared another marriage,
    With both their hearts so full of glee,
'I'll range no more in foreign countries.
    Now since Sophia has cross'd the sea.'

89   The Indian Lass

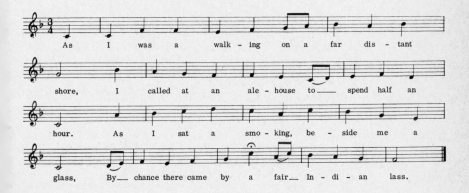

As I was a walk-ing on a far dis-tant shore, I called at an ale-house to spend half an hour. As I sat a smo-king, be-side me a glass, By chance there came by a fair In-di-an lass.

2 She sat down beside me and squeezed my hand.
  She said, 'You're a stranger, not of this land;
  I have fine lodgings if with me you'll stay:
  My portion you shall have without more delay.'

3 With a glass of good liquor she welcomed me in:
  'Kind sir, you are welcome to have any thing';
  But as I embraced her this was her tone:
  'You are a poor sailor and far from your home.'

4 We tossed and we tumbled in each other's arms,
  And all that long night I embraced her sweet charms;
  With rural enjoyment the time passed away:
  I did not go to leave her till nine the next day.

5 This lovely young Indian on the place where she stood,
  I viewed her sweet features and found they were good.
  She was neat, tall and handsome, her age was sixteen,
  She was born and brought up in a place near Orleans.

6 The day was appointed, he was going away,
  All on the wide ocean to leave her to stay;
  She said, 'When you're over your own native land,
  Remember the Indian that squeezed your hand.'

7 Early next morning we were going to sail;
  This lovely young Indian on the beach did bewail.
  I took off my handkerchief and wiped her eyes:
  'Do not go and leave me, my sailor,' she cries.

8 We weighèd our anchor, away then we flew
  With a sweet and pleasant breeze, and parted me from her
      view;
  But now I am over and taking my glass,
  So here's a good health to the young Indian lass.

The accommodating young lady represents a sort of pre-Hollywood and homely exoticism. The charming little tale is notable for its relaxed atmosphere and its 'rural enjoyment' (delightful euphemism).

A Scots laird loses his future bride to an English nobleman, but in a violent struggle takes her back on her wedding day. So run the earlier versions – though none is earlier than the late eighteenth century – of the ballad which Child calls 'Katharine Jaffray' (his no. 221), after the usual name of the heroine (if one so passive can be called a heroine). In later versions the contenders are separated not by nationality but by status. A squire turns the tables on a wealthy farmer, in a reversal of the well-loved theme of the lowly suitor triumphing over one of high degree. The ballad was widely known in Scotland, Ireland and England, as well as in North America. This version comes from the late Mrs Cecilia Costello, who was born in Birmingham of Irish parents, with some lines and phrases added from a broadside.

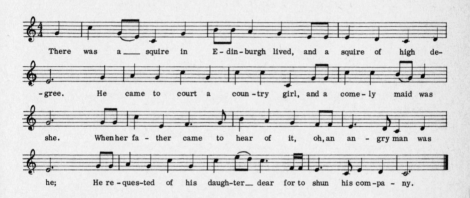

There was a squire in Edinburgh lived, and a squire of high degree. He came to court a country girl, and a comely maid was she. When her father came to hear of it, oh, an angry man was he; He requested of his daughter dear for to shun his company.

2 Now there was a farmer lived in the east, and he had one only
       son;
   He came to court this country girl till he thought he had her
       won.
   He got consent from her father and mother, from old and
       young likewise,
   But still she cries, 'I am undone,' whilst the tears rolled from
       her eyes.

3 She sent her love a letter and she sealed it with her hand,
   Saying, 'My dearest dear, I'm going to be wed unto a farmer's
       son.'
   Oh, the very first line that he read of it he smiled and this did
       say:
   'Oh, I will deprive him of his bride all on his wedding day.'

4 He sent her back an answer to be sure to dress in green,
  And a suit of the same he would put on to the wedding to
      repair:
  'Come dress yourself in green and I the same will wear,
  And I will wed with you, my dear, in spite of all that's there.'

5 Then he looked east and he looked west, and he looked all
      round his land;
  He mounted eight score of his men all of the Scottish clan.
  He mounted them all on a milk-white steed, and an angry
      man rode he;
  And away, away to Edinburgh went with his company
      dressed in green.

6 'You are welcome here, you are welcome here. Where have
      you been all day?
  And who are all these gentlemen that are riding out this way?'
  He laughed at them, he scoffed at them, he smiled, and this
      did say:
  'Oh, they must have been some fairy troop that rode along
      this way.'

7 They handed him a glass of wine, he drank to the company
      round,
  Saying, 'Happy is the man, the man they call the groom;
  But happier is the man,' he said, 'that will enjoy the bride;
  Another might like her as well, and take her from his side.'

8 Then up spoke the intended groom, and an angry man was he:
  'If it is for fight that you've come here, well, I am the man for
      thee.'
  'Oh, it's not for fight that I've come here, but friendship for to
      show,'
  Saying, 'Give me one kiss from your lovely bride, and away
      from you I'll go.'

9 He caught her by the lily-white hand and round the middle so
   small,
   He brought her out of the wedding house without the leave of
   all;
   He brought her out of the wedding house without the leave of
   me,
   And away, away to Edinburgh went with his company
   dressed in green.

91   The Flower of Serving Men

*Unusually, it is possible to give a precise date and authorship to this ballad. It
was written by the prolific balladeer, Laurence Price, and published in July
1656, under the title of 'The famous Flower of Serving-Men. Or, The Lady
turn'd Serving-Man'. It lasted in the mouths of ordinary people for three
hundred years: what a tribute to the work of any writer, leave alone the obscure
Laurence Price. Oral tradition, however, has made changes. The original has
28 verses and a fairy-tale ending: 'And then for fear of further strife,/He took
sweet William to be his Wife:/The like before was never seen,/A Serving-
man to be a Queen.'*

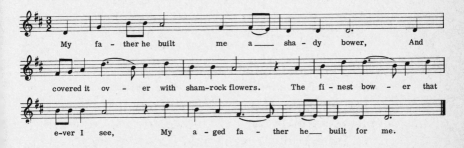

My father he built me a shady bower, And
covered it over with sham-rock flowers. The finest bower that
ever I see, My aged father he built for me.

2 My father he married me to a noble knight.
  My mother she owed me a dreadful spite;
  She sent nine robbers all in one night
  To rob my bower and slay my knight.

3 How could she have done me a bigger harm,
  To murder my babies all in my arms?
  Left nothing at all for to wrap them in,
  But the bloody sheets that my love died in.

187

4 All alone, all alone then I will wash them,
　All alone, all alone I will bury them;
　Cut off my hair and I'll change my name
　From Fair Eleanor to Sweet William.

5 I will saddle my horse and away I'll ride,
　And until I come to some fair king's side;
　And one of those servants I'll give a ring,
　To carry my message to the king.

6 It's 'Do you want either horse or groom,
　Or do you want any stableman?
　Do you want a manservant all in your hall
　To wait on the nobles when they do call?'

7 It's 'We don't want neither horse nor groom,
　Nor we don't want ne'er a stableman,
　But we wants a manservant all in our hall
　To wait on the nobles when they do call.'

8 Now on one day it did happen so
　That this young lord did a-hunting go,
　Left no one at home but this gay old man
　To keep company with Sweet William.

9 And when she found she was all alone,
　Took down a fiddle and played a tune:
　'Once my love was a rich, noble knight,
　And me myself was a lady bright.'

10 Oh, then by and by this young lord came home:
　'What news, what news, oh, my gay old man?'
　'Good news, good news, oh, my lord,' said he,
　'Your servantman is a gay lady.'

11 'Go and fetch me down, then, a pair of stays,
　That I might lace up her tender waist;
　Go and fetch down that gay gownd of green
　That I might dress her up like my queen.'

12 'Oh, no! Oh, no! Oh, my lord,' said she,
'Pay me my wages and I'll go free;
For I never heard tell of a stranger thing,
As a servantman to become a queen.'

The last line of verse 5 ('That I might dissolve a gracious thing'), and the first ('Then by and by this young lord went out') and second (wanting) of verse 8 have been replaced by lines from other versions.

Took down a fiddle: in Price's original, a lute.

92 The Watercress Girl

Even without a knowledge of the original street ballad, one would have to conclude that the style and sentiment of this song made it unmistakably Victorian.

One day I took a ram-ble___ down by a run-ning stream, Where the wa-ter li-lies gam-bol___ - it was a love-ly scene;___ And there I saw a mai-den, a mai-den from the dell: She was gath-'ring wa-ter-cres-ses 'twas Mar-tha, the wa-ter-cress girl.___ Then her hair it hung in tres-ses, down by the stream that's close to the mill; She was gath-'ring wa-ter-cres-ses, was Mar-tha the wa-ter-cress girl.

Chorus

189

2 I asked if she was lonely, she answered with a smile:
'Kind sir, I am not lonely, for here I daily toil.
I have to rise up early my cresses for to sell;
My Christian name is Martha – they call me the watercress
girl.'

3 The day is not far distant when Martha will be mine,
And on our wedding morning it will be nice and fine.
I'll have to rise up early and dress up like an earl,
To go and marry Martha, the sweet little watercress girl.

After verse 3, the last line of the chorus was varied to: 'Was my little watercress girl'.

93   The Bailiff's Daughter of Islington

Judging from the frequency of reprints, the ballad was immensely popular in the latter part of the seventeenth century. It has continued to be held in affection ever since, though one doubts the informant who told Child in the 1880s that it 'may be heard any day at a country cricket-match'. It has been confidently asserted that the Islington in question is the village in Norfolk, rather than the one formerly near London and now part of it.

There was a youth, a well be-lo - vèd youth, He was a squi - re's son; He loved a bai-liff's daugh-ter dear, She lived at Is-ling-ton.

2 But she was shy and never could
On him her heart bestow,
Till he was sent to London Town
Because he loved her so.

3 When seven years had passed away
She put on mean attire,
And straight to London she did go
About him to enquire.

190

4 But as she went along the road,
  The weather being hot and dry,
  She nestled on a mossy bank
  And her lover came riding by.

5 'Give me a penny, thou 'prentice boy,
  Relieve a maid forlorn.'
  'But before I give thee a penny, sweet one,
  Pray, tell me where thou wer't born.'

6 'Oh, I was born in Islington.'
  'Then, tell me if you know
  The bailiff's daughter of that place.'
  'She died, sir, long ago.'

7 'If she be dead, then take my horse,
  My saddle and bridle also,
  And I will to some far off land
  Where no one doth me know.'

8 'Oh, stay, oh, stay, thou goodly sir:
  She is standing by thy side;
  She's here alive, she is not dead,
  But ready to be thy bride.
  She's here alive, she is not dead,
  But ready to be thy bride.'

94   The Female Highwayman

Pris-cil-la on one sum-mer's day Dressed her-self up in men's ar-ray; With a brace of pis-tols__ by__ her side All for to meet her true love on the plain.
[she did ride]

2 And when she saw her true love there
  She boldly bade him for to stand.
  'Stand and deliver, kind sir,' she said,
  'For if you don't I'll shoot you dead.'

3 And when she'd robbed him of all his store,
  Said she, 'Kind sir, there's one thing more;
  The diamond ring I've seen you wear,
  Deliver that and your life I'll spare.'

4 'That ring,' said he, 'my true love gave;
  My life I'll lose but that I'll save.'
  Then, being tender-hearted like a dove,
  She rode away from the man she love.

5 Anon they walked upon the green,
  And he spied his watch pinned to her clothes,
  Which made her blush, which made her blush
  Like a full, blooming rose.

6 ' 'Twas me who robbed you on the plain,
  So here's your watch and your gold again.
  I did it only for to see
  If you would really faithful be.
  And now I'm sure that this is true,
  I also give my heart to you.'

True lovers, it seems, delighted in finding ways to test each other's constancy, and this little tale was very well loved. One suspects that it dates from the heyday of highwaymen in the mid-eighteenth century, though its first appearances in print were early in the nineteenth.

95   Pretty Peg of Derby, O

The tune of this ballad is much better known than the words. It was used for many songs, the best known being 'The Chesapeake and Shannon', which dates from 1812 and was still a favourite at Tom Brown's Rugby. 'Pretty Peg' probably dates from the 1780s. In some versions the haughty heroine is not a '*blooming maid*', but a chambermaid, and there is a final stanza in which the luckless captain dies of love: '*When they came to the town, to the very last town,/The town they call Kilkenny, O;/His name was captain Wade, and he died for a maid,/And he died for the pretty girl of Derby, O*'.

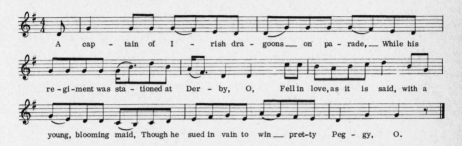

A cap-tain of I-rish dra-goons__ on pa-rade,__ While his re-gi-ment was sta-tioned at Der-by, O, Fell in love, as it is said, with a young, blooming maid, Though he sued in vain to win__ pret-ty Peg-gy, O.

2 'Tomorrow I must leave thee, pretty Peggy, O,
Though my absence may not grieve thee, pretty Peggy, O.
Braid up thy yellow hair, ere thou trip'st it down the stair,
And take farewell of me, thy soldier laddie, O.

3 'Ere the dawn's reveille sounds to march, I'm ready, O,
To make my pretty Peg a captain's lady, O,
Then what would your mammy think to hear the guineas
    clink,
And the hautboys playing before thee, O?'

4 'Must I tell you,' says she, 'as I've told you before,
With your proffers of love not to tease me more?
For I never do intend e'er to go to foreign land,
Or follow to the wars a soldier laddie, O.'

5 Out spake a brother officer, the gallant De Lorn,
As he eyed the haughty maiden with pity and scorn:
'Never mind, we'll have galore of pretty girls more,
When we've come to the town of Kilkenny, O.'

6 But when they had come to Kilkenny, O,
Where the damsels were lovely and many, O,
Sighing deeply, he would say, 'Though we're many miles
    away,
Let us pledge a health to pretty Peg of Derby, O.'

hautboys: oboes.

193

That a person should die for love already strains credibility, but that two should do so, and both in the same ballad, is going too far. Nevertheless, 'Lord Lovel' remained popular for over a hundred years (the earliest known version dating from 1770). At the same time, however, alongside straightforward versions, as Child tartly commented (his no. 75), 'a gross taste has taken pleasure in parodying it'.

Lord Lo - vel he stood at his ca - stle gate, Comb-ing his milk - white steed, When up came La - dy Nan - cy Bell To wish — her lo - vier good speed, speed, speed, To wish — her lo - vier good speed.

2 'O! where are you going, Lord Lovel?' she said.
'O! where are you going?' said she:
'I'm going, my Lady Nancy Bell,
Foreign countries for to see–e–e–
Foreign countries,' etc.

3 'When will you come back, Lord Lovel?' she said;
'When will you come back?' said she.
'In a year or two, or three, or four,
I'll come back to my Lady Nancee–e–e–
I'll come back,' etc.

4 He'd only been gone twelve months and a day,
Foreign countries for to see,
When languishing thoughts came into his head,
Lady Nancy Bell he would go see–e–e–
Lady Nancy, etc.

5 So he rode, and he rode, on his milk-white steed,
Till he came to London town;
And there he heard Saint Pancridge bells,
And the people all mourning around,
And the people, etc.

6 'O! what is the matter?' Lord Lovel he said;
'O! what is the matter?' said he:
'A Lord's lady is dead,' the people all said,
'And some call her Lady Nancee–e–e–
And some call her,' etc.

7 Then he order'd the grave to be open'd wide,
And the shroud to be turned down;
And then he kiss'd her clay-cold lips,
Whilst the tears came trickling down,
Whilst the tears, etc.

8 Then he flung his self down by the side of the corpse,
With a shivering gulp and a guggle;
Gave two hops, three kicks, heav'd a sigh, blew his nose,
Sung a song, and then died in the struggle,
Sung a song, etc.

9 Lady Nancy, she died as it might be to-day;
Lord Lovel, he died as to-morrow;–
Lady Nancy, she died out of pure pure grief;
And Lord Lovel, he died out of sorrow.
And Lord Lovel, etc.

10 Lady Nancy was laid in Saint Pancridge's church,
Lord Lovel was laid in the choir;
And out of her buzzum there grew a red rose,
And out of her lovier's a brier,
And out of her, etc.

11 So they grew, and they grew, to the church-steeple [top],
And they couldn't grow up any higher;
So they twin'd themselves into a true-lover's knot,
For all lovers true to admire,
For all lovers, etc.

Inside a Whitewashed Hospital

The cloying sentimentality of ballads like this was in vogue at the turn of the century.

In - side a white - washed hos - pi - tal An old man dy - ing lay._____ His face was hand - some, frank and true, His hair was tur - ning grey._____ 'Have you a wife?' the nurse she asked, 'No friend you wish to see?'_____ 'Ha, no,' he cried, 'I had a wife But she was too young for me._____ An old man's dar - ling was an old man's bride,_____ An old man's dar - ling was a sweet young bride._____ A youth came and won her;_____ they drif - ted far a - part._____ An old man's dar-ling broke an old man's heart.

2 The nurse drew near the old man's side.
As she listened to his tale
She smoothed his hair and softly said,
As her face grew strangely pale:
'Perhaps she went by some mistake,
And not for love she fled.'
'No, no, she was too young for me':
'Twas all the old man said.

3 The tears ran down the nurse's cheek,
Her arms around him threw:

'Dear Jack,' she cried, 'I am your wife,
That has been true to you.
They said you had another wife;
Too late I've found they lied.'
Early next morn both Jack and nurse
In death lay side by side.

VIII
Bound to be a Row:
Love and Marriage

98   A Noble Riddle Wisely Expounded

*'The Man in the Wilderness asked of me/"How many blackberries grow in the
sea?"/I answered him as I thought good,/"As many red herrings as grow in the
wood"'. Such riddles unfailingly provoke wonder and delight because of their*

verbal felicity, their symmetrical (if at times surrealistic) logic, and the deep sense of satisfaction which their resolution brings. Sequences of riddles frequently appear in folk narratives, in which the protagonists by a correct solution can either ward off some danger or achieve some positively beneficial outcome. In the earliest known version of the ballad given here (a manuscript of 1444 in English, but entitled in bad Latin, 'Inter diabolus et virgo'), a young women eludes the clutches of the devil by successfully answering his riddles. Our version (a street ballad issued in 1675) has retained its riddles but lost its supernatural quality: now, the correct solution merely gives the young woman the right to marry her knight. The erotic implications are emphasized by the first refrain line, for 'broom' here means the female private parts.

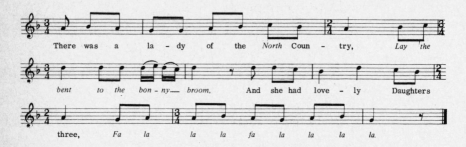

2 There was a Knight of Noble worth,
Which also lived in the *North*.

3 The Knight of courage stout and brave,
A Wife he did desire to have.

4 He knocked at the Ladies Gate,
One evening when it was very late.

5 The youngest sister she let him in,
And pin[n]'d the doore with a silver pin.

6 The second sister she made his bed,
And laid soft pillows under his head.

7 The youngest Daughter that same night
She went to bed with this young Knight.

8 And in the morning when it was day,
These words unto him she did say.

198

9 Now you have had you[r] will quoth she
   I pray sir Knight will you marry me?

10 The brave young knight to her reply'd,
    Thy suit fair Maid shall not be deny'd.

11 If thou canst answer me questions three,
    This very day will I marry thee.

12 Kind sir in love O then quoth she
    Tell me what your questions be.

13 O what is longer than the way?
    Or what is deeper than the Sea?

14 O what is louder than a Horn?
    Or what is sharper than a Thorn?

15 Or what is greener than the Grasse?
    Or what is worse than women was?

16 O Love is longer than the way,
    And Hell is deeper than the Sea.

17 And thunder's louder than a horn,
    And hunger's sharper than a thorn.

18 And poyson is greener than the grass.
    And the Divel is worse than woman was.

19 When she these questions answered had,
    The Knight became exceeding glad.

20 And having thoroughly try'd her wit,
    He much commended her for it.

21 And after as 'tis verify'd,
    He made of her his lovely Bride.

22 So now fair Maidens all adieu,
This Song I dedicate to you.

23 I wish that you may constant prove,
Unto the man that you doe [love].

99 The Widow that keeps the 'Cock Inn'

Public house landladies, it seems, have a great power of attraction. The landlady is also a widow, and a very desirable catch, in this gentle little tale from a street ballad (though beware of the sly wit in the last line).

A trav-'ler for ma-ny long years I have been, But I ne-ver went o-ver to France; Most ci-ties and all mar-ket towns I've been in, ___ From Ber-wick-on-Tweed to Pen-zance. Ma-ny ho-tels and ta-verns I've been in my time, And ma-ny fair land-la-dies seen, But of all the fair char-mers who o-thers out-shine, ___ give me the sweet wi-dow, the dear lit-tle wi-dow, I ___ mean the sweet wi-dow who keeps the *Cock Inn*.

2 There's Bet at the *Blossom* and Poll of the *Crown*,
Fat Dolly who owns the *Red Heart*;
There's Kate of the *Garter and Star* of renown
And Peggy who keeps the *Skylark*,
Spruce Fan of the *Eagle* and Nan of the *Bell*,
Pretty Jane of the *Man drest in Green*,
But of all the fair creatures who others excel,
Give me *etc*.

200

3 When last in her little bar parlour I sat,
  I joked her about her lone state:
  'A brood of young chickens, dear widow, mind that,
  Far better around you would prate.'
  Says she, 'Pray don't reckon afore they are hatched.'
  Says I, 'Where's the harm or the sin?
  You can manage a second, we're very well matched,
  Give me,' *etc.*

4 Then here's to the dear little charmer I prize
  In a bumper now filled to the brim,
  For who could resist such a pair of black eyes
  As in rich moisture they swim.
  Away then, away, with my batchelor's vow,
  My hand then in hers with the ring;
  For if she be willing to take me in tow,
  I'll marry the widow, the dear little widow,
  I'll marry the widow and keep the *Cock Inn*.

100   Magherafelt Hiring Fair

A widow who owns, not an inn, but a farm, here sets out to hire a labourer but finds a husband instead.

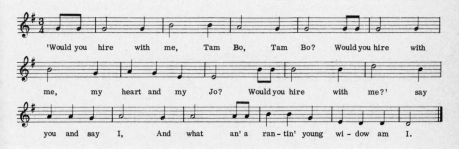

'Would you hire with me, Tam Bo, Tam Bo? Would you hire with me, my heart and my Jo? Would you hire with me?' say you and say I, And what an' a ran-tin' young wi-dow am I.

(Spoken) 'What wages, mistress?'

    2 'Two pounds five,' *etc.*
      (Spoken) 'Too little wages, mistress.'

3 'Then two pounds ten,' *etc.*
  (Spoken) 'What diet, mistress?'

4 'Sowans and eels,' *etc.*
  (Spoken) 'Too slippy diet, mistress.'

5 'Then potatoes and beef,' *etc.*
  (Spoken) 'Where will I lie, mistress?'

6 'You'll lie in the laft,' *etc.*
  (Spoken) 'The rats might eat me, mistress.'

7 'You'll lie wi' the weans,' *etc.*
  (Spoken) 'The weans might kick me, mistress.'

8 'Well, then we'll get married,' *etc.*

Magherafelt: in Nothern Ireland.   *weans*: children.
Sowans: pudding of oats and water.

101   Bill the Weaver

A husband arrives home to find his wife entertaining another man, whom he violently repulses. The subject is potentially grim, but it is treated with high good humour, though justice is undoubtedly done.

'Oh, mo-ther dear, I've just got mar-ried; Bet-ter had I long-er tar-ried, For my wife she does de-clare That the bree-ches she will wear.'

2 'Come, loving son, no more discover,
  I'll have thee go home and love her;
  Now give thy wife just what's her due,
  For I don't want no more of you.'

3 Now the neighbours they did tell him,
   For they all did want to please him:
   'I'll tell thee where and I'll tell thee now
   Who I saw with your wife, just now.

4 'We saw her with Bill the Weaver;
   They were very close together,
   On the footpath by the door,
   In they went, then we saw no more.'

5 Now he went home all in a wonder,
   Knocking on the door like thunder.
   'Who is there?' the weaver cried.
   'It is my husband, thee must hide.'

6 Up the chimney then he ventured;
   She opened the door and her husband entered.
   He searched the rooms and the chambers round.
   But not a soul could there be found.

7 Up the chimney then he gazèd,
   He stood there like one amazèd;
   There he saw that wretched soul,
   Perched on top of the chimney pole.

8 'Now, Bill the Weaver, I have got thee;
   I shall neither hang nor drown thee.
   I shall stifle thee with smoke.'
   Thus he thought, but he never spoke.

9 So he built up a roaring fire,
   Just to please his own desire;
   It made poor Bill to cough and sneeze,
   Where he sat at little ease.

10 As he stacked on more fuel,
   His wife said: 'I am your jewel;
   As long as I am your lawful wife,
   Please take him out and spare his life.'

11 There were never a black devil of a chimney sweeper
   Half as black as Bill the Weaver;
   Hands and face and clothes likewise:
   He sent him home with two black eyes.

102 The Fellow that Played the Trombone

The humour here stems from situation (the deception of the husband and his thwarted rage), incongruity and double entente.

2 Now she said she liked his music and she'd go there every
      week;
  I said it would be her downfall if she didn't stop her cheek.
  She took no notice what I said, and went from time to time,
  While I sat at home and nursed the kids while him and her did
      shine.
  On his *etc.*

204

3 The other night I woke and found she'd gone with all her
       clothes,
  She'd gone with that bandsman to a land that no one knows;
  And if I ever find her I'd break their honeymoon,
  I'd smash his bloody instrument if I catched him playing a
       tune.
  On his *etc.*

103   His Little Wife Was with Him
All the Time

I know a cer-tain Mis-ter Brown, a qui-et sort of gent, Whose

lit-tle wife was with him all the time; The

peo-ple used to laugh at him, for ev-'ry-where he went His

lit-tle wife was with him all the time. At

last he thought he'd like a change, so said to her one day, I've

got to go to Lon-don,dear, on busi-ness right a-way!' He

meant to go a-lone, and was sur-prised to hear her say, 'Your

lit-tle wife goes with you all the time!'

Chorus

Poor old Brown, when he came to town, He

did not seem to think it all sub-lime; For

oh, you know, wher-e-ver he chanced to go, His

1. lit-tle wife was with him all the time.

2. time.

2 Said he, 'I've only come to town on business, understand!'
   But his little wife was with him all the time.
   That business seemed to take him to a place they called the
        Strand,
   And his little wife was with him all the time.
   He tried his level best to get an hour on his own,
   And offered once to call a cab and send her home alone;
   But though he walked about till he was sore in every bone,
   His little wife was with him all the time.

3 His business seemed to lead him into every public bar,
   But his little wife was with him all the time.
   He went to see the ballet, thought, 'What lovely girls they
        are!'
   But his little wife was with him all the time.
   That night in bed a lovely vision rose before his mind –
   He dreamt he was the Sultan, and had wives of every kind;
   A cold foot brought him back to earth, and Brown woke up to
        find
   His little wife was with him all the time.

4 Poor Mr Brown was out of sorts, though why, I cannot say –
   For his little wife was with him all the time.
   A very sweet young damsel chanced to wink at him one day,
   And his little wife was with him all the time.
   Next morn they started homewards by the earliest of trains;
   He'd two black eyes, a broken nose, and felt all over pains;
   He never said who did it, but the simple fact remains
   That his little wife was with him all the time.

The News of the World *published this song in 1898, in a feature, 'Songs
that are Sung at Halls and Theatres', which continued to appear weekly for
some forty years. (Nostalgia is fed by an advertisement on the same page for
Bugle Brand Bottle Beers, 'from 2/6 per dozen'). The chromaticism of the
melody was a feature of music hall writing at the time.*

Bound To Be a Row

An abundance of popular narratives, both stories and songs, dwells with malicious glee on the discomforts and disasters of marriage. This one is from the husband's view-point.

I am an un-lu-cky mar-ried man, I've such an aw-ful wife; To please her I do all I can but still she plagues my life. If I do eve-ry-thing that's right she'll find a fault some-how, And if I just stay out all night there's bound to be a row. There's bound to be a row, there's bound to be a row; I do all my life to please my wife, but there's bound to be a row.

2 She wakes me in the morning in a very cruel way:
   She kicks me on the floor, and not a hard word do I say.
   I have to wash my stockings, my shirts and fronts I vow,
   And if I don't wash hers as well there's bound to be a row.

3 She takes in a lodger – he's single, bye the bye,
   And I've to make room for him and on the sofa lie.
   They give to me the bones and it doesn't seem right
         somehow,
   And if I just say half as much there's bound to be a row.

4 She sometimes makes a party to some friends to 'tain at night,
   And I've to hurry home from work to be in time to wait;
   And as they hustle me about if I don't scrape and bow,
   And say 'Yes, sir' and 'Thank you', 'Please', there's bound to
         be a row.

5 After I have earnt my wages after working hard all week
  I turn up every half-penny but then she's got the cheek
  To give me twopence to myself, and for that I've got to bow,
  And if I spend it all at once there's bound to be a row.

'tain: entertain.

105   A Woman's Work Is Never Done

A number of different ballads in the seventeenth and eighteenth centuries took this title and theme. The one given here was collected in Berkshire in 1907 by Cecil Sharp. Its message is unequivocal.

2 He said: 'You lazy huzzy, indeed you must confess,
   For I'm a-tired o' keeping you in all your idleness';
   But the woman she made him answer, saying: 'I work as hard
      as you,
   Then I will run just through the list what a woman has to do.

3 'Here's six o'clock each morning, off to your work you do go;
   Here's eight, arise and light the fire and the bellows for to
      blow.
   I have to set the tea things and get the kettle boiled;
   Besides, you know, I have to work, and dress the youngest
      child.

4 'Here's four times a day your wants for to employ,
   Here's breakfast, dinner, tea and supper we have to stew and
      fry.
   I have to shake and make the bed, and sweep the rooms also;
   I have to dust the windows and empty the chamber po'.

5 'Besides, you know I make it the rule to dress the little ones
                    and send them off to school.
   So men if you would happy be, don't grumble at your wife,
      so,
   But think on your poor mother, how she put up with you.

po': pot.

The first half of the second line of the fifth stanza is wanting in the original. The
appropriate bars of music should be omitted in singing.

106   Marrowbones

*Once again, the subject seems grim: a wife attempts to murder her husband, but
is murdered by him; and only a few years ago there were furious complaints
when the song was taught in a school. Yet the mood is one of expansive good
humour, the main interest is in a battle of wits, and only the most un-
imaginative could take the story literally. It is not quite clear how ground
marrowbones could have produced blindness, but there seems to have been a
belief that this was the case.*

Now there was an old wo-man in I - re - land, In
Ire - land she did dwell; ____ She loved her old
hus - band right dear - ly, And a - no - ther man twice as
Chorus
well. ____ To my rid - dy fol lol, ri rid - dy fol
lol, Ri rid - dy fol lau - rel day, Ri rid - dy fol
lol, ri rid - dy fol lol, Ri rid - dy fol lau - rel day.

2 So the old woman she went to the doctor's
To see what she could find;
She said she wanted something
That would turn the old man blind.

3 He said: 'Take thee sixteen marrowbones
And grind 'em up so small;
And when he's had 'em he'll be so blind
He won't see any at all.'

4 But the doctor he wrote a letter,
And sealed it with his hand;
He sent it to the old man,
To make him understand.

5 Says the old man, 'I'll drown myself,
Because I've lost my sight.'
Says the old girl, 'I'll go with you,
And see you do it right.'

6 Now as they were a-walking,
A-walking to the brim,
The old man he shoved down his foot,
And pushed the old girl in.

7 Good Lord, how she did holloa,
   Good Lord, how she did scream;
   The old man he picked up a pole,
   And he pushed her further in.

8 And now my song is ended,
   I've got no more to say;
   The old girl she got drowned,
   The old man can rejoice again.

107   Get Up and Bar the Door

As Bronson says, this narrative 'has been popular in Scotland and is known in various forms, fabliau or folk-tale, in many parts of Europe and the Near East.' The version given here was collected by the American, James M. Carpenter, in Scotland, in the 1920s or 1930s. The text is very close to that of the earliest known copy, which appeared in Herd's Ancient and Modern Scots Songs *in 1769.*

It fell up-on a Mar - tin-mas night, And a gay time it was then, O, When our good wife got pud-dins to mak, And she boilt them in a pan, O. *Chorus* The bar - rin' o' oor door, weel, weel,___ weel, And the bar-rin' o' oor door weel.___

2 The wind blew cauld fae north to sooth,
   It blew across the floor, O;
   Quo'd oor guidman to oor guidwife:
   'Get up and bar the door, O.'

211

3 'My hand is in my hussifkip,
    Guidman, as ye may see, O;
    Thoch it shouldna be barred this hunner year,
    It'll no be barred by me, O.'

4 They made a paction 'tween them twa,
    They made it firm and sure, O,
    Wha'e'er should speak the foremost word
    Should rise and bar the door, O.

5 But there cam' twa gentlemen
    At twal o'clock at night, O,
    And they could nather see hoose nor ha',
    Nor coal nor candlelight, O.

6 'Whether this be a rich man's hoose,
    Or whether it be a poor, O?'
    But ne'er a word would ane o' them speak
    For the barrin' o' the door, O.

7 First they et the white puddin's,
    And then they et the blak, O,
    And muckle thocht the guidwife to hersel',
    Though ne'er a word she spak', O.

8 The tane enti the ither said,
    'I'll tell ye what I'll dee, O:
    Ye'll tak' off the auld man's beard,
    And I'll kiss the guidwife, O.'

9 'There is nee water in the hoose,
    And what will we do then, O?'
    'What ails ye at the puddin' bree
    That's boilt enti the pan, O?'

10 Up then jumps oor guidman,
    And an angry man was he, O:
    'Wad ye kiss my wife afore my face,
    And scad me wi' puddin' bree, O.'

11 Up then jumps oor guidwife,
    Gi'ed three skips on the floor, O:
    'Guidman, ye've spoken the foremost word.
    Git up and bar the door, O.'

hussifkip: housewifery.   *bree*: broth.

108   The Cooper of Fife

The age-old problem of taming the shrew is solved by the threat of violence in this ballad which Child (his no. 277) called 'The Wife Wrapt in Wether's Skin'. It is strange that the cooper should have a 'gentle' (that is, noble) wife, but this explains why she will not or cannot work. To avoid the wrath of her kin the cooper proposes to beat not her, but his sheepskin laid over her. Beneath the surface may be the old taboo on the shedding of royal blood.

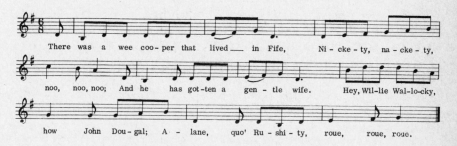

2 She wadna bake, nor she wadna brew,
    For the spoiling o' her comely hue.

3 She wadna card, she wadna spin,
    For the shaming o' her gentle kin.

4 She wadna wash, nor she wadna wring,
    For the spoiling o' her gowden ring.

5 The cooper's awa' to his woo' pack,
    And he's laid a sheep skin on his wife's back.

6 It's, 'I'll no thrash ye for your proud kin,
   But I will thrash my ain sheep skin.'

7 'Oh, I will bake and I will brew,
   And never mair think on my comely hue.

8 'Oh, I will card and I will spin,
   And never mair think on my gentle kin.

9 'Oh, I will wash and I will wring,
   And never mair think on my gowden ring.'

10 A' ye wha hae gotten a gentle wife,
   Send ye for the wee cooper o' Fife.

109   The Devil and the Farmer's Wife

The rejection by the devil of a termagant wife who terrorizes his demons has elements widely known both in Europe and the Orient. The ballad, however, is relatively modern, the earliest printed version ('improved' by Robert Burns from tradition) having appeared in 1792.

It's of an old far-mer as I've heard tell, Had a wi-cked old wife and he wished her in hell. With my tit-ty fa lol, whack fol de rol, Tit-ty fa lad-dle di, tit-ty fa lol; Tit-ty fa lol, whack fol de rol, Tit-ty fa lad-dle di, tit-ty fa lol.

2 The devil he came to the old man at plough,
   Saying, 'I want your wife and I'll take her now.'

3 'Oh, take my old woman with all my heart;
   I hope you and her will never more part.'

214

4 He shoved the old woman into a sack,
 And away he went with her slung on his back.

5 He tipped her out when he came to hell's gate,
 Saying, 'Here's an old woman who'll make me a mate.'

6 And all the young imps they raised up a din:
 'Oh, take her away, she'll do us all in.'

7 He shoved the old woman into a sack,
 And to the old farmer he took her straight back.

8 So ends the story and you'll all agree
 That women are worse than men ever could be.

110   Johnnie, My Man

A heavy drinker suddenly responds to his wife's appeal that their children are suffering: to everyone's benefit, he returns to teetotal domesticity. There is enough genuine warmth in the song to have made it widely popular in Scotland a hundred years ago, and it is still by no means forgotten.

'O, John-nie, my man, do ye no' think on ri-sin'? The day is far spent and the nicht's co-ming on; Ye're sil-ler's near dune and the stoup's toom be-fore ye, So rise up, my John-ny, and come a-wa' hame.'

2 'Wha's that at the door that's speakin' so kindly?'
 ' 'Tis the voice of your wifie, ca'd Jeanie by name.'
 'Come in by, my dearie, and sit down beside me,
 It's time enough yet for to gang awa' hame.'

3 'Don't ye mind on the time when we first fell a-courting?
   We had naething but love then to trouble our mind;
   We spent a' our time 'mang the sweet-scented roses,
   And I ne'er thocht it lang then to gang awa' hame.'

4 'O, weel dae I mind on the time that ye speak o',
   And weel dae I mind on yon sweet flowering glen;
   But thae days are a' past, and will never return, love,
   Sae sit down beside me, and I'll soon gang hame.'

5 'Don't ye mind on your bairns, they're a' at haem greetin'?
   There's nae meal in the barrel to fill their wee wames;
   While ye sit here drinkin', and leave me lamentin',
   O, rise up, my Johnnie, and come awa' hame.'

6 Then Johnnie rose up, and he banged the door open,
   Saying, 'Cursed be the tavern that ere let me in,
   And cursed be the whisky that's made me sae frisky.
   O, fare ye weel, whisky, for I'm awa' hame.

7 'And, Jeanie, my dear, your advice will be taken,
   I'll leave aff the drinkin' and follow thee hame,
   Live sober and wisely, and aye be respected,
   Nae mair in the ale-house I'll sit down at e'en.'

8 Noo Johnnie gaes out on a fine simmer's evening
   Wi' his wife and his bairnies fu' trig and fu' bien,
   Though no' long before that in rags they were rinnin',
   While Johnnie sat drinkin' in the ale-house at e'en.

9 Contended and crouse he sits by his ain fireside,
   And Jeanie, a happier wife there is nane;
   Nae mair to the ale-house at nicht he does wander,
   But he's happy wi' Jeanie and the bairnies at hame.

toom: empty.
mind: remember.
greetin': crying.
wames: bellies.

simmer: summer.
fu' trig and fu' bien: very trim and
   comfortable.
crouse: merry.

The Wild Rover

No doubt this is a good example of male chauvinism, with a husband after seven years' 'rambling and roving' magnanimously deciding to go back to his 'sweet loving wife', whom he expects to be still waiting for him. The ballad has nevertheless (or therefore) remained exceedingly popular, especially in a crowded bar after an evening's drinking. The words, published on broadsides in the nineteenth century, were perhaps inspired by 'The Green Bed', the ballad of a returning sailor who also feigns poverty to test the real worth of his hosts. The tune has the unique distinction among traditional airs of being employed in soccer chants.

2 I went to an alehouse where I used to resort;
  I began for to tell them my money was short.
  I asked them to trust me, their answer was: 'Nay,
  Such custom as yours we can have every day.'

3 My hands from my pockets I pulled out straightway
  With handfuls of gold for to hear what they'd say.
  'Oh, here's ale, wine and brandy, here's enough of the best,
  And all that we told you, it was but in jest.'

4 'Begone, you proud landlord, I bid you adieu:
  The devil a penny I'll spend more with you.'
  The money I've got, boys, I'll lay up in store,
  And I never will play the wild rover no more.

5 So now I'll go home to my sweet loving wife,
  In hopes to live happy all the days of my life.
  From rambling and roving I'll take better care,
  Unless poverty happens to fall to my share.

IX
Mark Well the Jest:
Merry Tales

112   **The Stark-naked Robbery**

Nudity (pace the naturists, but not excluding them) has been a perennial subject for broad humour (and even narrow humour). There is perhaps some basis in reality for this tale, since highwaymen not infrequently robbed their victims even of their clothes. Joseph Andrews suffered this fate in chapter 12 of Fielding's novel.

All you that are mer-ry both far off and near, Come lis-ten a-while and the truth you shall hear. A — co-mi-cal sto-ry as e-ver was known, It hap-pened not far from fair Wor-cester town. Gee ho, dob-bin, hi ho, dob-bin, Gee ho, dob-bin, gee up and gee ho.

2 A coach up from London did thither repair,
   And seated inside three fine ladies there were;
   And into the coach then I vow and protest
   Came three gallant gentlemen, mark well the jest.

3 When they came to Broadway the coachman espied
   Three highwaymen galloping side by side.
   They rode to the coachman and bid him to stand:
   'Deliver your money, then,' they did command.

4 They took money and watches and rings of great price,
   Then naked they stript men and ladies likewise;
   And naked together as when they were born
   They got in the coach for to keep themselves warm.

5 They buckled the curtains that no one might see;
   The coach drove along with this bare company.
   They'd not driven far when yet more highwaymen
   Rode up to the coachman and bid him to stand.

6 'They're all Adams and Eves, for to lie I do scorn,
   All naked within as when they were first born.'
   Believe him they would not so straight went to see,
   Then smiled and said: 'We'll make an Adam of thee.'

7 They stepped up to the coachman without fear or doubt:
   'They're Adams within, you'll be Adam without.'
   They stript him stark naked and bare to the skin:
   'You'll not make such game of your charges again.'

8 He drove to the town and he rode to the inn.
   On seeing him naked the ostler begin
   To call Sue and Mary to view all his fare,
   And they through their fingers began for to stare.

9 The ostler and groom clothed the gentlemen,
   And Mary brought clothes that the ladies put on.
   So now to conclude as the truth I declare,
   Poor Mary fell in love with the coachman's ware.

Broadway: village near Evesham in Worcestershire.

The Lobster

This mock-tragic tale goes back at least to 1610, when it appeared in Béroalde de Verville's Le Moyen de Parvenir, *a symposium in which all sorts of grave personages of antiquity exchange Rabelaisian jokes and anecdotes. The song has been sung under a variety of titles, but seldom printed. Bishop Percy had an extremely rude version, 'The Sea Crabb', which remained unpublished until 1868, when Furnivall included it in his supplement of* Loose and Humorous Songs *from Percy's manuscript, not without the invocation of* Honni soit qui mal y pense. *Our version was recorded as recently as 1974–75.*

2 'Oh, yes,' said the fisherman, 'I've got two;
   One is for you and the other is for me.'

3 I took the lobster home, I put it in the dish;
   I put it in the dish where the misses used to wish.

4 First I heard her grunt, then I heard her scream;
   There was the lobster a-hanging on her front.

5 The missus grabbed a brush and I grabbed the broom;
   We chased the bloomin' lobster round and round the room.

6 Now the moral of my story, the moral is this,
   Always have a shufti before you have a wish.

shufti: look.

The Cunning Cobbler

With the words 'Done Over' added to the title, this boisterous bedroom farce is not uncommon on broadsides. The humour is both broad and sly, and rough justice prevails in the end, after a good deal of fast-moving action.

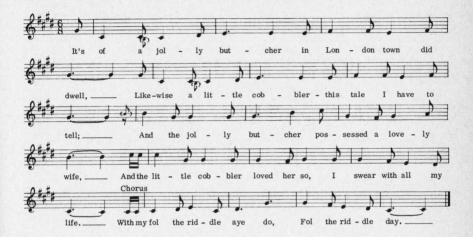

It's of a jol-ly but-cher in Lon-don town did dwell, ____ Like-wise a lit-tle cob-bler-this tale I have to tell; ____ And the jol-ly but-cher pos-sessed a love-ly wife, ____ And the lit-tle cob-bler loved her so, I swear with all my life. ____

Chorus

With my fol the rid-dle aye do, Fol the rid-dle day. ____

2 The butcher went to market all for to buy an ox,
   And the little cobbler, sly as any fox,
   Dressed all in his Sunday clothes, a–courting he did go,
   All with the jolly butcher's wife because he loved her so.

3 And when the little cobbler stepped in the butcher's shop,
   The butcher's wife knew what he meant and she bade him to
        stop.
   He said, 'My little darling, have you anything for me?'
   And she, all smiling at him, said, 'I'll go upstairs and see.'

4 She went up to the bedroom and gave the snob a call:
   'I've got a little job for you if you've brought your awl;
   And if you do it workmanlike some money I shall pay.'
   'Oh, thank you,' said the cobbler, and he quickly stitched
        away.

5 And as he was a–stitching a knock come at the door;
   The cobbler crawled beneath the bed and lay down on the
        floor.

'Lay still,' says the butcher's wife, 'what will my husband
    say?'
And then she let the policeman in along with her to play.

6 The butcher come from market and put them in a fright;
The policeman quickly run downstairs and soon was out of
    sight.
The butcher's wife so nimbly locked up the bedroom door,
And in her fright she quite forgot the cobbler on the floor.

7 And at night the butcher was lying in the bed:
'There's something in here very hard,' unto his wife he said.
She said, 'It is my rolling pin.' The butcher gave a laugh:
'How come you dare to roll your dough all with a
    policeman's staff?'

8 The butcher flung the truncheon underneath the bed;
It broke the chamber pot to bits and cracked the cobbler's
    head.
The cobbler shouted, 'Murder.' Says the butcher, 'Who are
    you?'
'I am the little cobbler who mends a lady's shoe.'

9 'If you are the little cobbler just come along with me.
I'll pay you out for mending shoes before I've done with
    thee.'
He locked 'im in the bullock yard; the bull began to roar;
The butcher laughed to see 'im toss the cobbler o'er and o'er.

10 Early next morning when the people were about,
The butcher rubbed his face in blood and let the cobbler out;
He pinned a paper on his back and on it was the news:
'The cobbler to the bedroom goes to mend the ladies' shoes.'

11 The cobbler was so frightened, he ran with all his might;
His coat and breeches were all torn, he looked an awful sight.
His anxious wife did meet him and he shouted out, 'Oh,
    Lor','
He said, 'My dear I never will go stitching any more.'

snob: cobbler.

115 The Auld Wife and the Peat Creel

The device of hoisting a lover in a basket to reach his inamorata – or rather its appearance in literature – dates back to the fourteenth century. However, the ballad version of the tale does not appear to have been printed before the early nineteenth century, perhaps because of its uninhibited gusto. Child accepted it into his collection (no. 281) with reluctance because he believed that one passage 'which need not be particularized' was 'brutal and shameless almost beyond example'.

The far - mer's daugh - ter gade to the mar - ket Some white fish for to buy. The__ young squire fol - lowed af - ter her As hard as he could hie, ri-ca-doo, Tun - un - nay, ri-ca - doo, Tun -un - nay, ri-ca - doo a dee a day, Raddle ri-ca-doo, Tun - un - nay.

Chorus

2 'A gude mornin' to you, sweetheart,' she said;
   'For to see you I am richt glad,
   But my faither he locks the door every nicht,
   Puts the key below his head.'

3 'But ye maun get a long ladder
   That's thirty feet and three,
   And ye maun gang to the chimney top,
   And your brither will let you to me.'

4 He has got a lang ladder
   That is thirty feet and three;
   He has gane to the chimney top,
   And his brither lute him down in the creel.

5 But the auld wife she could nae rest,
   For thoughts ran in her head:
   'I'll lay my life,' quo' the silly auld wife,
   'There's a man in our dochter's bed.'

223

6 The auld man he rose up himsel'
   To see if it was true,
   But she tuke the young squire in her arms,
   And the curtains around him drew.

7 'Gude morrow to you, auld faither,' she said,
   'Whar are ye gaun sae soon?
   Ye disturbit me of my prayer,
   And so did ye last noon.'

8 'O woe to you,' he said,
   'And an ill death may you die.
   It was the braid book she had in her arms:
   She was preyand for you and me.'

9 But the auld wife she could nae rest
   Till she got up hersel',
   But sumthing or anither tuke the auld wife's fit:
   Into the creel she fell.

10 The man upon the chimney top
   He gade the creel a pou':
   'I'll lay my life,' quo' the auld wife,
   'The de'il will hae us aw just now.'

11 The man upon the chimney top,
   He lute the creel down fa';
   He brake three of the auld wife's ribs,
   Knock't her agane the wa'.

12 O the brume and the bonnie, bonnie broom,
   And the broom that I like weel,
   An every auld wife that's jealous o' her daughter,
   May be dangled in the same peat creel.

creel: basket.   '*O woe to you*': i.e. to his wife.
lute: let.   *broom*: see note, no. 98.

116   The Ragged Beggarman

A beggar who is given lodging in a stable seduces the daughter of the house, but all ends (relatively) well because he turns out to be a nobleman in disguise. Thus 'The Jolly Beggar' (Child no. 279), but it has many variants. Here, the woman fully expects the beggar to be a gentleman, and is furious when this turns out not to be so.

It's of a rag-ged beg-ger-man came trip-ping o'er the plain. He came un-to a far-mer's door, a lodg-ing for to gain.

Chorus
Ro-bel-low, zan-ga-la, Ro-bel-low, be-low, be-low.

2 The farmer he came out to view, he looked the man around;
   Says he, 'For a ragged beggarman, no shelter here is found.'

3 Then down the stair came the daughter fair, and viewed him
      cheek and chin,
   And said, 'He is a handsome man, I pray you take him in.'

4 The maiden bade him to the barn and made a bed with hay;
   She made it plumb and easy that the beggar there might lay.

5 She went into her father's house, she brought him cake and
      wine;
   She gave him of her father's clothes, all laced rich and fine.

6 The father laughed a mocking laugh: 'Thou art a silly fool
   To feed and clothe a beggarman that fasts and lyeth cool.'

7 She rose so early in the morn to unbar the linney door,
   And there she saw the beggarman a-standing on the floor.

8 He caught the maiden in his arms and to the bed he ran.
   'Now fie, for shame,' the maiden said. 'Thou art a forward
      man.'

225

9 She lay as still as any mouse, as if she had been dead;
   He gave her kisses two and three, and stole her maidenhead.

10 'I'm sure thou art no beggarman, of gentlemen art one,
   For you have spoiled an honest maid, and I am quite
             undone.'

11 'I am no squire, I am no lord, of beggars I be one;
   And beggars they be robbers all: by such you are undone.'

12 'I took you for a nobleman, I took you for a squire;
   In truth thou art the finest lad that runneth in the shire.

13 'My mother she will loudly chide, my father curse and ban,
   That I have played the fool this day all with a beggarman.'

14 She took the bed all in her hands and dashed it o'er the wall,
   Saying, 'Go you with the beggar man, my maidenhead and
             all.'

linney: barn.

117   The Pretty Chambermaid

*This is a beautifully balanced little song, rather like a dance. The word
'kissing' is almost certainly euphemistic.*

Not far from town a coun-try squire, an o-pen-hear-ted
blade, Had long con-ceived a strong de-sire to kiss his cham-ber-
-maid. One sum-mer's morn, quite full of glee, he led her to the
shade, And all be-neath the mul-berry tree he kissed his cham-ber-maid.

2 The parson's spouse from a window high this amorous pair
surveyed,
And softly wished, none can deny, she'd been kissed like the
chambermaid.
When all was o'er young Betty cried: 'Kind sir, I'm much
afraid
That woman there will tell your bride you've kissed your
chambermaid.'

3 The squire conceived a lucky thought that she might not
upbraid,
And instantly the lady brought where he'd kissed the
chambermaid.
All beneath the mulberry tree her ladyship was laid,
And three times three well kissed was she, like to the
chambermaid.

4 Next morning came the parson's wife, for scandal was her
trade:
'I saw your squire, madam, on my life, kissing your
chambermaid.'
'When?' cried the lady. 'Where and how? I'll soon discharge
the jade.'
'Beneath the mulberry tree, I vow, he kissed your
chambermaid.'

5 'This falsehood,' cried her ladyship, 'shall not my spouse
degrade.
It was I came there to make a sly, and not my chambermaid.'
Both parties parted in a pet, not trusting what was said,
And Betty keeps her service yet, that pretty chambermaid.

118   Jack the Jolly Tar

Another form of substitution is practised here, with a tarry sailor taking the place of a squire. In the earliest printed version (eighteenth century) the sailor took a merchant's place in the bed of a brazier's daughter. The lively ballad seems to have remained popular throughout the nineteenth century, and is today enjoying a new lease of life in folk song clubs.

O,— I am Jack and a jol - ly tar, O. Let— me re - turn from the sea so far, O. O,— I am Jack and a jol - ly tar, Let— me re - turn — from the sea so far.

Chorus
Fal la la doo, fal lal le - ro, Right fal la la doo.

Var.(a)
V.2 onwards

2 As I was walking through London city
  I found myself all in great pity,
  For I heard them say as I passed by:
  'Poor Jack all in the streets must lie.'

3 The squire courted for his fancy
  A merchant's daughter whose name was Nancy,
  And I heard them agree as I passed by,
  That night together for to lie.

4 'Oh, tie a string unto your finger,
  And let it hang out of the window;
  And I will come and touch the string,
  And you will come down and let me in.'

5 'Blame me,' said Jack, 'if I don't venture;
  I'll touch the string that hangs to the window.
  And Jack he went and touched the string,
  And she come down and let Jack in.

6 Next morning soon as she was wakened,
  She looked like one that was forsaken,
  For to see Jack lie with [his] check shirt,
  And almost covered all over with dirt.

7 'Oh, then,' said she, 'how came you here, O?
  I'm afraid you've robbed me of my squire, O.'

'No, no,' said Jack, 'I touched the string,
And you came down and let me in.'

8 'While it is so it makes no matter,
For Jack's the lad I'll follow after.
For I do love Jack as I love my life,
And I do intend to be Jack's wife.'

9 The squire come [by] all in a passion,
Saying: 'Curse the women through the nation,
For there is not one that will prove true,
And if there is 'tis very few.'

119   The London 'Prentice

Servants were great buyers of ballads, it is said, which might explain why they figure so often as ballad heroes. This wily 'prentice and his stratagem appear to have come straight out of the racy world of Tom Jones and Moll Flanders, though the ballad was taken down from a country singer in the early twentieth century.

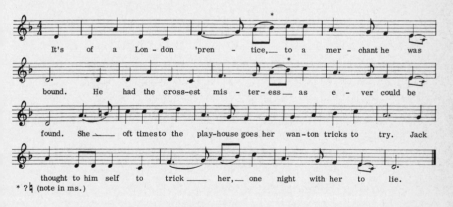

It's of a Lon - don 'pren - tice,— to a mer - chant he was bound. He had the cross-est mis - ter-ess— as e - ver could be found. She — oft times to the play-house goes her wan-ton tricks to try. Jack thought to him self to trick — her,— one night with her to lie.

* ? ♮ (note in ms.)

2 He hired a suit of clothing callèd rich or fine;
For to trepan his mistress it was his heart's design.
All with his knotted wig, his sword beside and all,
He goes down to the tavern and for a miss did call.

3 He had not been there but a little while when a knock or two
    he gave,
  When down came the drawer, saying, 'Kind sir, what will
    you have?'
  'It's a nice miss I want, sir,' the young man did reply.
  'That you shall have immediately to sit down by your side.'

4 Three pictures there were brought to Jack, all for to choose his
    miss.
  'Here is my own dear mistress,' thinks Jack, 'I will have this.'
  His misteress was sent along, so impudent and bold.
  She sat down by her 'prentice: not him did she behold.

5 She'd not been there a little while when Bow bells began to
    ring.
  She clasped his hand and said: 'Oh, is this not a pleasant thing?
  Is not this [a] pleasant thing,' said she, 'for now Bow bells do
    go.
  I love to hear them tolling, and so do you, I know.'

6 Now time being passing over, Jack hastened home with speed
  To take his suit of clothing to the right owner indeed.
  He'd not been home a little while when his mistress came in,
  But a little did she think where her Jack and she had been.

7 She'd not been home a little while, she began to storm and
    scold.
  She fixed Jack Parsons by the ears; he cried: 'Hold, my
    mistress, hold.
  Hold, hold your tongue, don't scold no more, for now Bow
    bells do go;
  I love to hear them tolling and so do you, I know.'

8 'O, fie, you saucy Jack, how could you trepan me so?
  I would not for five thousand pound your master he should
    know.
  It would make his heart so heavy and he would look so sad,
  'Twould fill his mind with jealousy, I'm sure he will go mad.'

9 Instead of kicks and scars she many kisses gave;
    She slipped a guinea into his hand, saying, 'More than this you
        shall have,
    If you will counsel keep and never confess at all,
    You shall have money when you please and I'll be at your
        call.'

Bow bells: euphemism (*encore et toujours*).

120   The Cluster of Nuts

*A Liverpool 'prentice proves at least as wily and much more manly than his
London counterpart. This is a very rare song, which survived as a tune with a
fragment of words which Stephen Sedley married to a broadside text* (The
Seeds of Love, *1967, p. 74). He aptly comments: 'It is a marvellous piece of
folk wit, with its deliberately transparent euphemisms about 'kissing', its play
on the business of Jack putting nuts into his mistress' apron and riding on his
master's mare (stanzas 10 and 11), and the neat piece of psychological detail in
stanzas 7 and 8. It is this, in fact, and not the nonsensical calculation, which is
the nodal point of the narrative.'*

2 He was proper, tall and handsome,
    And everything being right,
    He said he could sleep with a pretty girl,
    And kiss her twelve times a night.

3 His mistress being standing by,
    And hearing him say so,
    She says, 'Jack, I'll hold a wager
    That you don't perform it so.

4 'Five pounds is the wager,
    And twelve times is the bet;
    And I myself will be the judge
    When we are both in bed.'

5 His master being from home that night,
    And everything being right,
    He slipped into bed to his mistress,
    And kissed her twelve times that night.

6 Now one of them being drowsy,
    Which there was no virtue in,
    It caused his mistress for to say:
    'The wager I did win.'

7 'If I didn't win the wager,
    As I suppose you'd like,
    I'll leave it to my master
    When he comes home at night.'

8 'Be off, you saucy fellow.
    Would you let your master know?'
    'Indeed, upon my honour, ma'am,
    I do intend it so.'

9 When his master he came home that night,
    And at his supper sat,
    Says Jack unto his master:
    'Sir, I'm like to lose a bet.

10 'As your wife and I was walking
    Down by the greenwood side,
    And I upon your mare's back,
    A cluster of nuts I spied.

11 'I said there were twelve of them;
    She said there were eleven.
    Then I shoved them in her apron,
    And there were five and seven.'

12 'Five and seven is a dozen,
   As I've heard people say;
   So, Jack, you won the wager,
   And your mistress must you pay.'

13 His mistress being standing by,
   And hearing him say so,
   She clinked down the wager,
   And was glad to get off, you know.

14 When his master is from home
   She continually stuffs his guts;
   And she claps him on the shoulder.
   Saying, 'Jack, remember the nuts.'

121   The Stone Cutter's Boy

It's of a stone cutter's boy was returning from his work, A young damsel appeared in his sight, And he said, 'My dearest dear, If one moment you'll stay here, I will tell you what I dreamed of last night, of last night, I will tell you what I dreamed of last night.

2 [Oh, she turned herself round and she made a dead stop:
  'Your dreams are all fables, I know.
For the milking of my cow I cannot stay now,
So it's, pray you, young man, let me go.']

3 It was under an oak where we sat ourselves down;
  The trees they were fresh and green;
And what we did amiss I will leave you all to guess:
  She had the contents of my dream.

4 Then she picked up her pail, the cows for to milk,
   And so nimbly she tripped over the plain.
   She said: 'My dearest sweet, the next time we do meet,
   We'll repeat those dreams over again.'

*Here is another apprentice hero, in another piece of erotic wishful thinking.
Other versions have 'a bricklaying boy' or 'a young brickster', so the song
seems firmly linked with the building trade.*

122   The Buttercups All Grow

*Compared with the deft touches of 'The London 'Prentice' and 'The Cluster of
Nuts', this has a very angular gait. Nevertheless, the preposterous incidents
and the boisterous fun of the 'Buttercups' have their own appeal. The singer,
George Spicer, learned the song from a now-forgotten record in the 1920s.*

Now Mary Green loves me and I love her too We
blush when we meet like all true lovers do. Beside the plantation where
green meadows run We spoon in the dark and we have lots of fun,
Chorus (Slower)   Solo
Down in the fields where the buttercups all grow. My sweetheart said I was too
bashful and slow But she changed her mind when I let myself go.
Chorus   (a)   ossia (a)
Down in the fields where the buttercups all grow.

2 We walked side by side through the long, winding grass;
  The rhubarb grew sideways, the lettuce bolt fast.
  We walked 'neath the trees and the birds up above
  Were all busy dropping their tokens of love,
  Down in the fields where the buttercups all grow.

My girl climbed a gate and said, 'Turn your head, Joe,'
But I had a stiff neck so we let matters go,
Down in the fields where the buttercups all grow.

3 The birds were all greeting the day newly-born:
The sheep's in the meadow, the cow's in the corn;
But when sheep and cows have been round there a bit,
Well, it's not a nice place for a lady to sit,
Down in the fields where the buttercups all grow.
A cow licking Mary's face tickled her so;
She thought it was me and said, 'Don't slobber, Joe,'
Down in the fields where the buttercups all grow.

4 My sweetheart and I were behind a haystack
When a bumblebee flew down the small of her back.
Well, I saw what happened and in my distress
I pushed my right hand down the back of her dress,
Down in the fields where the buttercups all grow.
My hand down her back when she struck me a blow;
Now I'd no idea that bee was so far below,
Down in the fields where the buttercups all grow.

5 A ten gallon cask on the top of the hill
Came rushing towards us, my heart it stood still,
But Mary stood bravely, unflinching, 'tis true:
Her legs were that bandy that the barrel run through,
Down in the fields where the buttercups all grow.
Our courtship was swift and our honeymoon slow;
Our bed was so small that we both had to go,
Down in the fields where the buttercups all grow.

123   **Morgan Rattler, Or,**
        Darby O'Golicker

Sexual prowess is a frequent theme in balladry. When men of certain occupa-
tions are involved, such as ploughmen, mowers, weavers and tinkers, the
protagonists appear in their own right, but at the same time the tools and skills
of their trade are exploited metaphorically. The hammer man (blacksmith) is
too good an opportunity to miss.

Great boast ing of late___ I've heard of a feat, Of a
co - mi - cal blade___ called Mor - gan Rat - tler, But one's come to town___ will
soon cut him down, And he goes by the name___ of Dar - by O' Go-li-cker; A
no - ted young blade,___ a black-smith by trade,___ Well known by the la - dies to
be a great fro-li-cker, The la - dies do cry when they see him pass by, ___ 'There
goes the old ham - mer - man, Dar - by O' Go-li- cker.'

2 His music excels all coral and bells,
   His strokes more sweet than the warbling chorister;
   No flute or guitar can ever compare
   To the musical hammer of Darby O'Golicker.
   His excellent physic is good for the phthisic,
   'Twill cure their ills like a portion of jallap, sir;
   No doctor with pills can cure them so well
   As the essence extracted from Darby O'Golicker.

3 At Mullingar Fair young Jerry was there
   With Nancy Adair, that sweet pretty frolicker.
   Her gown she did pledge for the triangular wedge
   That was drove by the sledges of Darby O'Golicker.
   This maiden so fair with a languishing air,
   Her neck it was white, her hair it was yellow, sir;
   But being distresst she begged a request
   Of the blast from the bellows of Darby O'Golicker.

4 This ma'am did advance with an amorous glance;
   Straightway to a tavern he quickly followed her.
   On the table she told ten guineas in gold,
   Her anvil to pelt with his Darby O'Golicker.
   So now to conclude, pray don't think me rude,
   Now I've sung you a song of this gay frolicker.

236

Ah, who, oh, Morgan may sleep, here's the boy that can
  sweep
Twelve thirteeners off with his Darby O'Golicker.

phthisic: consumptive.
jallap: medicine.

thirteeners: English shilling (worth
    thirteen pence in Ireland at one time).

124   The Jolly Tinker

'Roome for a joviall tinker' was registered in 1675. Its fourteen verses tell the story of a gentleman who dresses as a tinker at the invitation of a married lady in order to mend her 'coldron' in her bedroom without arousing her husband's suspicion. By 1719–20 the tinker was operating in his own right, and the song was five verses down and entitled 'The Travelling Tinker, and the Country Ale-Wife: Or, the lucky mending of the leaking Copper', when it appeared in Tom d'Urfey's famous collection, Pills to Purge Melancholy *(5 vols.). The song then seems to have disappeared from print until the 1950s, when it emerged shorter, ruder, and with a certain class consciousness. This version can be heard on* Sing, Say and Play *(Topic Records 12TS275, 1978).*

Bring out your pans and ket-tles, my i-rons are all hot; Bring
out your pans and ket-tles and the holes I will all stop. With my
Chorus
rangs, tangs, ham-mers, nip-pers, pin-chers, Un-der the rose and o-ver the
mountains we will go, With a rang, tang, fol the rid-dle day.

2 Now he strolled into the kitchen and then into the hall,
  Taking off his coat and jacket, saying, 'Morning, ladies all,'
  With his *etc.*

3 Now she took the tinker upstairs to show him what to do,
  She laid herself upon the bed and so did the tinker, too,
  With his *etc.*

237

4 I've been a tinker for this last eight years or more,
  But I'm buggered if I blocked up such a rusty old hole before,
  With my *etc.*

125   The Quarry Bank Mashers

*The words 'masher' (flirtatious dandy) and 'on the mash' (courting) date this
song from the last years of the nineteenth century. It was made popular on the
halls by the brothers Malone, and has since turned up in traditional style with
various localities inserted: Ashton, Belfast, Bristol, Bury and Rochdale have
all figured, as well as Quarry Bank (Staffordshire).*

238

2 Now last night to a ball we're invited,
   To a ball and two ladies were there;
   Their cheeks were in bloom like the roses in June,
   They made such a lovely pair.
   We were dancing and singing till midnight,
   With the ladies we had all the fun;
   And after the dancing was over
   We had whisky, bananas and rum.

Alternative version of second verse:
Last Saturday night we were invited
To the *Roebuck* by two ladies fair;
Their cheeks were in bloom like the roses in June
As we danced with that beautiful pair.
There was dancing and singing till midnight,
We had whisky tobacco and rum;
And after the dancing was over
With those ladies we had lots of fun.

126   The Bush of Australia

*Oddly enough, this exotic ballad has come to light only in East Anglia.
Perhaps it was a local man's pipe dream. Walter Pardon, the singer of this
version, recalls that it was banned in public houses at one time. This was no
doubt not because of the general mood of genial sensuality, but the implications
of verse 4 and the conclusion of verse 5.*

2 I had not been long in that beautiful scene,
   Where the fields are delightful, the trees ever green,
   When a lovely young damsel to me did appear,
   From the banks of the river she quickly grew near:
   She's a native of happy Australia she's a native of happy
      Australia,
   Where, *etc.*

3 She took off her clothes and before me she stood,
   As naked as Venus just come from the flood.
   She looked me in the face and smiling, said she:
   'This is the robe that Dame Nature gave me
   On the day I was born in Australia, on the day I was born in
      Australia,
   Where,' *etc.*

4 She leapt in the water without fear or dread,
   Her beautiful limbs she quickly outspread;
   Her hair hung in ringlets, her colour was black;
   She said, 'You can see how I swim on my back
   In the streams of my native Australia, in the streams of my
      native Australia,
   Where,' *etc.*

5 Being tired of swimming she came to the brink:
   'Assistance,' said she, 'or surely I'll sink.'
   Like lightning I flew, took her out by the hand;
   I put out my foot, she fell down on the sand,
   And I entered the bush of Australia, then I entered the bush of
      Australia,
   Where, *etc.*

6 We sported together in the highest of glee
   In the fairest Australia that ever could be.
   My head on her beautiful breast was inclined,
   Till the sun in the west all its glories resigned,
   Then I left this fair maid of Australia, then I left this fair maid
      of Australia,
   Where the maidens are handsome and gay.

SOURCES AND NOTES

Appended to the Source of each song (if appropriate) is a note of its classification in F. J. Child, *The English and Scottish Popular Ballads*, 5 vols, 1882–98; reprinted 1965, or G. M. Laws, *American Balladry from British Broadsides*, Philadelphia, 1957.

1 Who Hung the Monkey?
Written by Ned Corvan (1830–65) to the tune of 'The Tinker's Wedding'. Text: Hartlepool Public Library. Tune: R. Ford, *Vagabond Songs and Ballads of Scotland*, Paisley, 1904, p. 1.

2 The Congleton Bear
Written in 1972 by Peter Coe.

3 The Doctor Outwitted by the Black
Text: broadside printed by P. Breton, Exchange Street, Dublin (Cecil Sharp Broadside Collection, Vaughan Williams Memorial Library). I have corrected the spelling and made a few minor alterations. Tune: sung by Ezra Barhight, Avoca, New York, USA; collected by Ellen Steckert, 15.4.1956 (K. S. Goldstein and R. H. Byington, *Two Penny Ballads and Four Dollar Whiskey*, Hatboro, Pennsylvania, 1966, pp. 22–3).

4 The Private Still
'Air and words of this favourite song supplied by Mr William Carton, retired NST, Garryduff, Ballymoney, who heard Daniel moore sing it 40 years ago' [i.e., c. 1890] (No. 103 in the Sam Henry Collection, *Songs of the People*, which was published in the *Northern Constitution* newspaper, Coleraine, between 1923 and 1939. Sam Henry, a Customs and Excise official by trade, lived from 1878 to 1952). The text can also be found a broadside printed by Disley of London (Crampton Collection, vol. 8, p. 278, British Library 11621 h. 11).

5 Wha's Fu'?
Tune and text of the first five verses, under the title of 'I'm Jolly Fu' ' in *Miscellanea of the Rymour Club*, Edinburgh, vol. 2, 1912–19, pp. 120–1. The remaining verses have been added from G. R. Kinloch's *Ancient Scottish Ballads*, 1827. The whole can be heard on *The Clutha* (Topic 12TS242, 1974).

6 Sandy Dawe
Communicated by Christine Briggs (née Cunningham) of Birmingham, who lived in Ayrshire as a child in the 1950s, and learned the song from her grandmother. After 'began to sail', her version continues: ' 'Twas like a rat without a tail./When the rat began to run,/'Twas like a man without a gun.'

7 Paddy and the Whale
Sung by Tommy Dempsey on the record, *Green Grow the Laurel* (Leader LER 2096, 1976).

8 The Christmas Hare
Written by Roger Watson in 1966.
9 Lancashire Dick
Text: broadside without imprint (Baring Gould Collection, vol. 5, p. 251, British Library LR 271 a. 2). Tune: I believe that 'Gee ho dobbin' was intended, and I have used a version from J. Stokoe and S. Reay, *Songs and Ballads of Northern England*, Newcastle and London, n.d. (1899), p. 84.
10 Dixie's Dog
Written by Bernard Wrigley in 1970, and sung by him on *The Phenomenal B. Wrigley* (Topic 12TS211, 1971).
11 The Pear Tree
Sung by Frank Hinchliffe on the record, *Sheffield Park* (Topic 12TS308, 1977); recorded by Mike Yates and Ruairidh and Alvina Greig, July, 1976.
12 The Three Merry Travellers
Text: broadside printed by C. Bates, at the Sun and Bible in Pye Corner (J. W. Ebsworth (ed.), *The Bagford Ballads*, vol. 1, 1878, p. 51). Tune: W. Chappell, *Popular Music of the Olden Time*, 1859, p. 506.
13 O'Reilly and Big MacNeil
Written by Donneil Kennedy; sung by Geordie McIntyre on *The Streets of Glasgow* (Topic 12TS226, 1973).
14 The Old Woman and Her Pig
Sung by Sam Bennett (1865–1951), Ilmington, Warwickshire; collected by James M. Carpenter (No. 238, Carpenter Collection, Library of Congress).
15 The Wife of Usher's Well
Sung by 'Mrs Annie Kidd, Ivy Cottage, Glen Ythan, Rothienorman, Scotland. Learned from sister, Annie Bannerman, Upper Rashie Slack, Ythan Wells, sixty-five years ago. Had not seen in print. Sister, while spinning, sang a hundred songs without stopping' (No. 50, Carpenter Collection). Child no. 79.
16 Cold Blows the Wind
Text: 'Sent first by Mrs Gibbons da. of late Sir W. P. Trelawney Bart. as she remembered it sung by her nurse Elizabeth Dodge, in & abt. 1828. She did not recall verses 5. 6. 10. 11 – supplied by J. Woodrich, Blacksmith, Woolacot Moor, His version of v. 3 ran: When a twelvemonth and a day were up,/The body straight arose/"What brings you weeping o'er my grave/That I get no repose?" ' (S. Baring-Gould MSS, Plymouth Central Library). Neither Mrs Gibbons' manuscript, nor the full text of Woodrich's version, has survived. Baring-Gould believed that there was a further, forgotten verse, after v. 12. He published an abbreviated version of this text in *Songs of the West*, with a tune from an unidentified source. Woodrich's tune has been used here ('taken down from J. Woodrich, Thrushleton by S. B. G., 1889'). Child no. 78, 'The Unquiet Grave'.
17 The Lover's Ghost
P. W. Joyce, *Old Irish Folk Music and Songs*, Dublin 1909, p. 219. Learned by Joyce during his childhood in Glenosheen, County Limerick. Child no. 248, 'The Grey Cock, or, Saw You My Father?'
18 The Holland Handkerchief
Sung by Packie Byrne (b. 1917) on *Songs of a Donegal Man* (Topic 12TS257,

1975); recorded by Tony Engle and Mike Yates, 1974. Child no. 272, 'The Suffolk Miracle'.

19 The Cruel Ship's Carpenter
Tune and verses 4, 5 and 8 (substantially): sung by George Dunn (1887–1975), Quarry Bank, Staffordshire; collected by Roy Palmer, 21. 6. 1971 (*Folk Music Journal*, 1973, p. 289). Remainder of text from a broadside printed by Bloomer of Birmingham. Laws P 36.

20 The Cruel Mother
Sung by Elizabeth Wharton, a gipsy, in Shropshire; collected by C. S. Burne, 13. 7. 1885, and published in her *Shropshire Folk-lore*, 1883–86, pp. 540 and 651. Child no. 20.

21 Molly Bawn
As no. 18. Laws O 36.

22 The Grey Selkie
Sung by James Henderson (b. 1903), South Ronaldsay; collected by Alan Bruford, 170–2 (*Tocher*, no. 26, 1977, pp. 97–9). Verse 14 is a combination of the last two verses of the original, omitting the prefatory words, '. . . you've done . . .'. Child no. 113, 'The Great Silkie of Sule Skerry'.

23 The Twa Magicians
A. Sung by Miss Bell Duncan, Lambhill, Inch, Scotland (No. 283, Carpenter Collection). B. Peter Buchan, *Ancient Ballads and Songs of the North of Scotland*, 1828. Child no. 44.

24 The Maid on the Shore
Tune and verse 6: Joyce, p. 152. Remainder: communicated by Martyn Briggs. Laws K 27.

25 Tam Lin
Sung by Betsy Johnston on *The Muckle Sangs* (Tangent TNGM 119/D, 1975); recorded in Glasgow by Ailie Munro and Hamish Henderson, 1974. Child no. 39.

26 The Miner's Dream
Sung by Mrs Lucy Woodall (1894–1979), Old Hill, Cradley Heath, Worcestershire (formerly Staffordshire); collected by Roy Palmer, 6.1.1979.

27 The Well below the Valley
Sung by John Reilly (c. 1926–70) of County Roscommon; collected by Tom Munnelly, 1969 (B. H. Bronson, *The Singing Tradition of Child's Popular Ballads*, Princeton, New Jersey, 1976, pp. 83–5. The transcription of tune and variants is by Professor Bronson, and appears in the same place). John Reilly can be heard singing the ballad on *The Bonny Green Tree* (Topic 12T359, 1978). Child no. 21, 'The Maid and the Palmer'.

28 The Cherry Tree Carol
Sung by J. Thomas (b. 1848), Camborne, Cornwall; collected by Cecil Sharp, 9. 5. 1913 (*Journal of the Folk Song Society*, vol. V, 1914, pp. 11–13). Child no. 54.

29 Sir Patrick Spens
Sung by James ('Black Jimmie') Mason, Stonehaven, Scotland (Nos 180 and 182, Carpenter Collection). Child no. 58.

30 The Mistletoe Bough
Written by Thomas H. Bayly (words) and Henry R. Bishop (tune) in the

early 1830s. Text: broadside printed by J. Ringham, 50 Steep Hill, Lincoln (A Collection of Ballads, British Library 1876 e. 3), and also many other printers. Tune: J. L. Hatton and E. Faning (ed.), *Songs of England*, Boosey, n.d., vol. 3, pp. 44–9.

31 Lord Thomas
Sung by Harriet Dowley and others, Edgmond, Shropshire; collected by G. A. Jackson, 1872 (Burne, pp. 545–6 and 651). 'Some unimportant verses' omitted by the collector because 'they may be found in all good collections' have been restored in square brackets from Child (no. 73 D), who calls it 'Lord Thomas and Fair Annet'.

32 Barbara Allen
Sung by Frank Hinchcliffe (for whom, see no. 11); collected by Mike Yates, 5. 7. 1976. Child no. 84, 'Bonny Barbara Allan'.

33 Andrew Lammie
Sung by Sheila MacGregor on *The Muckle Sangs* (for which, see no. 25); recorded in Blairgowrie by Peter Cooke and Hamish Henderson, 1974. Child no. 233.

34 Lord Gregory
Sung by Mrs Gillespie, Glasgow, who learned the song from a girl companion in Buchan in the middle of the nineteenth century: collected by Gavin Greig, 1905 (G. Greig and A. Keith, *Last Leaves of Traditional Ballads and Ballad Airs*, Aberdeen, 1925, pp. 60–3). Child no. 76, 'The Lass of Roch Royal'.

35 The Betrayed Maiden
Text: broadside printed by Pitts, Toy and Marble Warehouse, 6 Great St Andrew Street, Seven Dials (C. H. Firth, *An American Garland*, Oxford, 1915, pp. 69–71). Tune: under the title of 'His Mother Standing', in *Journal of the English Folk Dance and Song Society*, vol. 3, p. 244. The same tune was also used for 'The Cruel Mother'. Laws M 20, 'Betsy is a Beauty Fair'.

36 The Swan Swims So Bonny
Tune and verses 1–6, 8–10 and 15: 'sung by an Irishman, in Liverpool'; collected by Frank Kidson (JFS II, 1906, p. 285). Remainder of text: verse 7: from a manuscript (marked no. 22) in the Gilchrist Papers (Cecil Sharp House); verses 11–14: from Scott's *Minstrelsy*, vol. II, 1802, p. 143. Child no. 10, 'The Two Sisters'.

37 The Sheffield Apprentice
John Ord, *The Bothy Songs and Ballads of Aberdeen, Banff & Moray, Angus and the Mearns*, Paisley, 1930, pp. 421–2. Laws O 39.

38 Little Montgrove and Lady Barclay
Sung by Miss Bell Duncan (for whom, see no. 23) (No. 283, Carpenter Collection). Child no. 81, 'Little Musgrave and Lady Barnard'.

39 Green and Yellow
Learned by me from Tony Seymour of Kidderminster, Worcestershire. Child no. 12, 'Lord Randal'.

40 The Poor Little Fisher Boy
Tune and first verse: sung by William Wickham, Blackham, Sussex; collected by A. G. Gilchrist, May, 1907 (JFS VIII, 1931, p. 38). Remainder of text from a broadside printed by H. Such, 23 Union Street, Borough, London (Frank Kidson MSS, Mitchell Library).

41 Rambling Robin
Text: broadside without imprint in Bradford Public Library. Tune: untraced.

42 The Lambton Worm
Communicated by Keith Gregson of Sunderland. The song dates from the 1860s.

43 Dilly-dove
Sung by Mrs E. Goodwin. Weobley, Herefordshire; collected by Mrs E. M. Leather (1876–1928) and notated from a phonograph record by R. Vaughan Williams (E. M. Leather, *The Folk-lore of Herefordshire*, Hereford and London, 1912, p. 204). Child no. 18, 'Sir Lionel'.

44 Long John, Old John and Jackie North
Written by Martin Carthy, and sung on his record, *Because It's There* (Topic 12TS389, 1979); based on 'Lang Johnny More' (Child no. 251).

45 The 'Golden Vanity'
Sung by Johnny Doughty (b. 1903) of Brighton on his record, *Round Rye Bay for More* (Topic 12TS324, 1977); recorded by Mike Yates, 1976. Child no. 286, 'The Sweet Trinity (The Golden Vanity)'.

46 Robin Hood and the Bishop of Hereford
Sung by George Stone, Wareham, Dorset, who learned it sixty years before; collected by H. E. D. Hammond, November, 1906 (JFS III, 1907, p. 61). Child no. 144.

47 Johnnie o' Braidisleys
Sung by Alex Mackay, butcher, Alford; collected by Gavin Greig (G. Greig and A. Keith, *Last Leaves of Traditional Ballads*, Aberdeen, 1925, pp. 93–5). Child no. 114, 'Johnie Cock'.

48 McPherson's Rant
Sung by Jimmy McBeath (1894–1971) on his record, *Wild Rover No More* (Topic 12T173, 1967).

49 The Draggletail Gipsies
Sung by Mrs Overd, Langport, Somerset; collected by Cecil Sharp, 4. 8. 1904 (C. Sharp and C. L. Marson, *Folk Songs from Somerset*, first series, 1904, p. 18). Child no. 200, 'The Gypsy Laddie'.

50 The Female Sailor
Sung by Henry Burstow, Horsham, Sussex; tune collected by Lucy Broadwood, 1. 1. 1894; text sent on by Henry Burstow (both in Broadwood Papers, Cecil Sharp House). Laws N 3, 'Female Sailor Bold'. I am indebted to Keith Gregson for the Sunderland newspaper cutting.

51 Grace Darling
Sung by Thomas James Tarrant (b. 1885), Woodbridge, Suffolk; collected by George Ewart Evans, 15. 7. 1968. A similar version can be heard on Walter Pardon's *Our Side of the Baulk* (Leader LED 2111, 1977).

52 The Proud Tailor
Sung by Sam Bennett (for whom, see n. 14) (No. 237, Carpenter Collection).

53 The Rambling Royal
Learned by me from Phil Colclough, formerly of Liverpool, now of Crewe. Laws J 15, 'James Ervin'.

54 Erin-go-Bragh
Ford, p. 49. Laws Q 20, 'Duncan Campbell'.

55 Lambkin
'Noted from Mr Alexander Crawford, of Leck, Ballymoney, who learned it fifty years ago when a boy at the Garry Bog, from an old travelling woman who made the children's flesh creep with this sinister song' (No. 735, Sam Henry Collection; published in *Songs of the People: selections from the Sam Henry Collection*, Part 1, ed. John Moulden, Blackstaff Press, Belfast, 1979, p. 81). Child no. 93, 'Lamkin'.

56 Mrs Dyer, the Baby Farmer
Collected by E. J. Moeran (*The Week-end Book*, 1929, p. 280); no further details available.

57 Young Henry Martin
Sung by Phil Tanner (1862–1950), Llangennith, Gower, on Columbia CA 16052–2, 1937. Child no. 250, 'Henry Martyn'. See also Child no. 167, 'Sir Andrew Barton'.

58 The Bold 'Princess Royal'
Sung by Bob Hart (1892–1978), Snape, Suffolk, on the record, *Flash Company* (Topic 12TS243, 1974); recorded by Tony Engle, September, 1973. Laws K 29.

59 Jack Donahue
Sung by Mr Ned Costello, Birmingham; collected by Roy Palmer, 1971 (*English Dance and Song*, vol. XXXVII, no. 3, 1976, p. 100). Laws L 22.

60 Heather Jock
Ford, pp. 131–5.

61 The Parson's Peaches
Written by Peter Bellamy of Norwich, and sung on his record, *Tell It Like It Was* (Leader LER 2089, 1975).

62 Young Johnson
Text: broadside printed by T. Bloomer of Birmingham (Birmingham Reference Library), and also by Ryle of Seven Dials, Marshall of Newcastle, and no doubt others. Tune: 'Dives and Lazarus' (L. E. B. Broadwood, *English County Songs*, 1893, p. 102). The tune is not indicated on the broadside, but evidence for its use to these words comes from oral tradition, for which see F. Purslow, *The Wanton Seed*, 1968, under 'Young Johnson'.

63 The Highwayman Outwitted
Sung by Mrs Kate Thompson, charwoman, Knaresborough, Yorkshire; collected by Frank Kidson, November, 1891 (JFS I 1904, p. 236). Laws L 2.

64 Jack Williams the Boatswain
Tune and first verse: sung by Alfred ('Butcher') Hoar, Hillingdon Union, Middlesex; collected by Cecil Sharp, 20. 9. 1913 (JFS VIII, Part 31, 1927, p. 13). Remainder of text: broadside printed by Pitts, 6 Gt Saint Andrew Street, Seven Dials (Quarto Street Ballads, Harding Collection, Bodleian Library). Laws L 17, 'Jack Williams'.

65 The Sewing Machine
Tune: sung by Woodcock, *Greyhound*, Scole, Nr Diss, Norfolk; collected by Ralph Vaughan Williams, 20. 12. 1911 (Vaughan Williams Add. MSS 54187, 8vo C, p. 32, British Library); marked 'words no use'. Text: broadside 'Sung by Mr George Harding' and printed by T. Pearson, 6 Chadderton Street, off Oldham Road, Manchester (Kidson Broadside Collection, Mitchell Library).

66 The Slap-bum Tailor
Text: broadside (slightly adapted) printed by T. Bloomer, Birmingham.
Tune: Roy Palmer, based on 'Old Farmer Buck'.
67 Limbo
Sung by James Brooman, Upper Faringdon, Hampshire; collected by G. B.
Gardiner, October 1908 (F. Purslow (ed.), *Marrowbones*, 1965, p. 53).
68 The Unfortunate Lad
Text: broadside printed by J. Ross, Arcade, Newcastle (A Collection of
Ballads, 1876 e., BL). The word 'Lock' in the first line has been deleted by the
printer, and a blank space left. Tune: under the title of 'The Unfortunate
Rake' (Crosby's *Irish Musical Repository*, c. 1808, p. 158). Laws Q 26, 'The
Bad Girl's Lament'.
69 Prosser's Betting Shop
Written by Dennis O'Neill (D. O'Neill and P. Meazey (ed.), *Broadsides:
Topical Songs of Wales*, Cardiff, 1973, p. 25).
70 Off to Epsom Races
Sung by George Attrill, Fittleworth, Sussex; collected by Bob Copper, 1954
(Bob Copper, *Songs and Southern Breezes*, 1973, pp. 208–9; see also pp.
73–82). In verse 4, the phrase 'all on one Derby day' has been used from
another performance by George Attrill instead of 'the sights they were so
gay', in the book.
71 All for the Grog
Sung by George ('Tom') Newman, Clanfield, Oxfordshire, on the record,
When Sheep-shearing's Done (Topic 12T254, 1975); recorded by Mike Yates,
1972–4.
72 Such a Nobby Head of Hair
Text: broadside 'Sold at Dalton's, 96 Walmgate, York' (York Publications,
1870 c. 2, no. 663, British Library). Tune: Gatty MSS, Birmingham Reference Library.
73 Jock Hawk's Adventures in Glasgow
Ord, pp. 278–9. The tune and chorus have been added from the Clutha's
record, *Scotia* (Argo ZFB 18, 1971).
74 Maggie May
Well known.
75 Ratcliffe Highway
Sung by James Knights (b. 1880), Woodbridge, Suffolk, on the record, *Sing,
Say and Play* (Topic 12TS375, 1978); recorded by Keith Summers.
76 Down by the Dark Arches
Sung by Walter Pardon on his record, *Our Side of the Baulk* (Leader LED
2111, 1977); recorded by Bill Leader, 1974.
77 The Bold Cockney
W. Christie, *Traditional Ballad Airs*, 2 vols, Edinburgh, 1876 and 1881, vol. 2,
p. 246. 'This Air and Ballad was a great favourite of the Editor's maternal
grandfather, and is here given exactly as he sung it. The Editor has not found
it hitherto published' (Christie's note).
78 Rosemary Lane
Sung by Mrs Lucy Woodall (for whom, see no. 26); collected by Roy Palmer,
16. 8. 1976.

79 The Fair Maid of Islington

Text: broadside with the subtitle of 'Or, The London Vintner Over-reach'd', 'Printed by and for W. D., and are to be sold by the Booksellers of *Pye-Corner* and *London-bridge*', Ebsworth, *Bagford Ballads*, vol. I, pp. 410–13 (II, 113, in original collection in British Library). Tune: 'Caper and Jerk It', otherwise known as 'Under the Greenwood Tree', in the Ashmole MSS, c. 1634 (C. Simpson, *The British Broadside Ballad and its Music*, New Brunswick, New Jersey, 1966, p. 724).

80 Little Ball of Yarn

Sung by Geoff Ling (b. 1916) on the record, *Singing Traditions of a Suffolk Family* (Topic 12TS292, 1977); recorded by Keith Summers, 1974–5.

81 The Ledbury Parson

Sung by Charlie Clissold (b. 1908), Brookthorpe, Gloucestershire; collected by Mike Yates and Gwilym Davies, 30. 3. 78; cf. the broadside, 'The Frolicsome Parson Outwitted' (Charles Hindley, *Curiosities of Street Literature*, 1871).

82 Poison in a Glass of Wine

Sung by Mrs Valerie Chapman (daughter of George Dunn), Quarry Bank, Staffordshire; collected by Roy Palmer, 1971. Laws P 30, 'Oxford City'.

83 There Was a Lady All Skin and Bone

JEFDSS, 1941, vol. IV, p. 43, from G. Petrie, *Ancient Music of Ireland*, 1855, p. 166.

84 The Magpie Said, 'Come In'

As no. 14; 'From an old banjo picker, Ilmington, 48 or 49 years ago.'

85 Amang the Blue Flowers and the Yellow

Sung by Mrs Gillespie (cf. no. 34), Glasgow; learnt in Buchan from her father's stepmother; collected by Gavin Greig (Greig and Keith, p. 25). Child no. 25, 'Willie's Lyke-Wake'.

86 The Banks of Sweet Dundee

Text: broadside printed by Harkness of Preston, no. 79 (Madden Collection, Cambridge University Library). Tune: *Newcastle Weekly Chronicle* Notes and Queries, 8. 10. 1892, contributed by Charles Ling of Dublin. Laws M 25, 'The Banks of Dundee'.

87 Blackberry Fold

Text: under the title of 'Squire and Milkmaid or Blackberry Fold', broadside without imprint (Ballads LR 271 a. 2, vol. 1–2, p. 103, British Library). Tune: sung by George Hill, East Stonham, Suffolk; collected by E. J. Moeran, 1921 (JFS VIII, Part 35, 1931, p. 269). Laws O 10, 'Pretty Betsy the Milkmaid'.

88 Lord Bateman

Text: broadside without imprint (Kidson MSS). Tune: sung by a Shropshire woman who learned it near Shrewsbury as a child; collected by Frank Kidson, 5. 1. 1899 (JFS I, Part 5, 1904, p. 240); words not taken down but 'practically the same as ordinary Ballad Sheet' (note in MS). Child no. 53, 'Young Beichan'.

89 The Indian Lass

Text: broadside printed by H. Such, 177 Union Street, Boro', S.E. (Kidson MSS). Tune: from Charles Lolley (F. Kidson, *Traditional Tunes*, Oxford, 1891, p. 111).

90 The Squire of Edinburgh
Sung by Mrs Cecilia Costello (1883–1976), Birmingham; collected by Roy Palmer, 1971; collated with broadside text printed by H. Such, 123 Union Street, Borough (Quarto Street Ballads, Harding Collection). Mrs Costello's song was recorded in 1951 for the BBC Sound Archive (BBC 17031: front) and appears, under the title of 'There was a squire in Edinborough lived', on her record, *Cecilia Costello* (Leader LEE 4054, 1975). Child no. 221, 'Katherine Jaffray'.

91 The Flower of Serving Men
Sung by Albert Dee (b. 1850), Bartley, Hampshire; collected by J. F. Guyer, 17. 12. 1908 (*Folk Music Journal*, 1967, pp. 147–8). A broadside, written by Lawrence Price in 1656, entitled 'The famous Flower of Serving-Men. Or, The Lady turn'd Serving-Man', is no. 111 in the Euing Collection (Glasgow University Library). Child no. 106, 'The Famous Flower of Serving-Men'.

92 The Watercress Girl
Sung by George Dunn (for whom, see no. 19); collected by Roy Palmer, 24. 5. 71 (*Folk Music Journal*, 1973, pp. 292–3).

93 The Bailiff's Daughter of Islington
Sung by Freda Palmer, Witney, Oxfordshire on the record, *When Sheepshearing's Done* (Topic 12T254, 1975); recorded by Mike Yates, 15. 10. 1972. Child no. 105.

94 The Female Highwayman
Sung by Mr J. Francis (b. 1902), Castle Bromwich, Warwickshire; collected by Roy Palmer, 24. 1. 1974 (*English Dance and Song*, vol. XXXVI, no. 2, Summer, 1974, p. 61). Mr Francis learned the song while a child in Norwich from his grandmother, a Norfolk woman. Laws N 21.

95 Pretty Peg of Derby, O
Text: *Notes and Queries*, 1st Series, vol. 6, 1852, p. 343, from Thomas Lyle's *Ballads and Songs*, 1827, p. 62; cf. slip-song without imprint in the Madden Collection, 6/1586. Tune: F. Kidson, 'Notes on Old Tunes', *Leeds Mercury*, 1891.

96 Lord Lovel
Davidson's Universal Melodist, n.d., vol. I, p. 148. Child no. 75.

97 Inside a Whitewashed Hospital
Sung by Mrs Lucy Woodall (for whom, see no. 26); collected by Roy Palmer, 6. 1. 1979.

98 A Noble Riddle Wisely Expounded
Text: broadside entitled 'A Noble Riddle wisele Expounded: Or, The Maids answer to the Knights three Questions', printed 'for F. Coles, T. Vere, and W. Gilbertson' in 1675 (Euing Collection, no. 253). Tune: 'Lay the Bent to the Bonny Broom' (T. d'Urfey, *Pills to Purge Melancholy*, 1719–20, vol. IV, p. 129, as amended by Bronson, 1976, p. 3). Child no. 1, 'Riddles Wisely Expounded'.

99 The Widow that Keeps the 'Cock Inn'
Text: broadside without imprint in V. de Sola Pinto and A. E. Rodway, *The Common Muse*, 1965, no. 147 (with two verses omitted). Tune: adapted from 'Jan's Courtship' (S. Baring-Gould, *Songs of the West*, 1905, no. 31, p. 64).

100 Magherafelt Hiring Fair
No. 748, Sam Henry Collection; 'collected in Tobermore'.

101 Bill the Weaver
Sung by 'Buster' Mustoe, Badsey, Hereford and Worcester; collected by Mike Yates, 12. 8. 1977. Laws Q 9.

102 The Fellow that Played the Trombone
As no. 75.

103 His Little Wife Was with Him All the Time
Written and composed by Walter P. Keen and Frederick W. Leigh; sung by Katie Lawrence (*News of the World*, 17. 4. 1898).

104 Bound To Be a Row
Sung by Jimmy McBeath (for whom, see no. 48) on his record of the same title, (Topic 12T303, 1978); recorded by Peter Hall, 1971.

105 A Woman's Work Is Never Done
Sung by William Hitchman (b. 1840), Faringdon, Berkshire; collected by Cecil Sharp, 1. 8. 1907 (*English County Songs*, vol. IV, 1920, p. 170).

106 Marrowbones
Sung by James Knights (b. 1880), Woodbridge, Suffolk; collected by George Ewart Evans, March, 1968. Previously published in my *Love Is Pleasing*, 1974, with verses 3 and 4 added from elsewhere.

107 Get Up and Bar the Door
Sung by 'James Christie, 41 Newton Hill, Scotland' (No. 178, Carpenter Collection). Child, no. 275.

108 The Cooper of Fife
Sung by Mrs Gillespie, Glasgow, 1905; learned from her father (Bronson, 1976, pp. 467; from Duncan MSS). Child no. 277, 'The Wife Wrapt in Wether's Skin'.

109 The Devil and the Farmer's Wife
Sung by Walter Pardon, Knapton, Norfolk; collected by Mike Yates, 24. 6. 1978. Child no. 278, 'The Farmer's Curst Wife'.

110 Johnnie, My Man
John Ord, *The Bothy Songs and Ballads of Aberdeen*, 1930.

111 The Wild Rover
Text: adapted from John Ashton, *Modern Street Ballads*, 1888, p. 353. Tune: well known.

112 The Stark-naked Robbery
Text: broadside printed by Harkness of Preston, no. 18 (Madden Collection). Tune: 'Gee ho, Dobbin' seems to fit very well, though it is not indicated. I have used the version from Chappell (p. 691), though that for no. 9 would do equally well. A traditional tune for the ballad was collected by Percy Grainger in 1906, under the title of 'The Coach to London' (*Folk Music Journal*, 1974, p. 336), but it is not very good, nor does it fit the broadside words.

113 The Lobster
Sung by Percy Ling (b. 1906); otherwise as for no. 80.

114 The Cunning Cobbler
As for no. 109; collected on 25. 6. 1978.

115 The Auld Wife and the Peat Creel
Sung by Mrs Storie, Lochwinnoch; learned from her brother, Tam; collected by Andrew Crawfurd, 12. 12. 1826 (Andrew Crawfurd MS, Paisley Central Library; published in E. B. Lyle, *Andrew Crawfurd's Collection of Songs*,

Edinburgh, 1975, no. 25, p. 64, and Bronson, 1976, p. 486. Child no. 281, 'The Keach in the Creel'.

116 The Ragged Beggarman
Sung by J. Gerrard, Collyhole, Chagford, Devon; text taken down by S. Baring-Gould, 1889, and melody by F. W. Bussell, October, 1890 (Baring-Gould MSS). The same text was known by another singer, William Setter, a moorman from Dartmoor, with a different tune, and this version is sung by Cyril Tawney on *Down Among the Barley Straw* (Leader LER 2095, 1976).

117 The Pretty Chambermaid
Text: broadside without imprint (A Collection of Ballads, 1876 e. 3, BL). Tune: adapted from 'William Guiseman' in Christie, vol. II, p. 172.

118 Jack the Jolly Tar
Sung by William Nott, Meshaw, Devon; collected by Cecil Sharp, 12. 1. 1904 (JFS II, Part 6, n.d. (1904 or 1905), pp. 38–9). Laws K 40; cf. broadside, 'The Merchant's Courtship to the Brazier's Daughter. An Old Song' (Madden Collection 5/1110).

119 The London 'Prentice
Sung by Mrs Verrall, Horsham, Sussex; collected by Ralph Vaughan Williams, 6. 9. 1908 (Vaughan Williams MS I 260).

120 The Cluster of Nuts
Text: broadside without imprint (though probably printed by Disley of London) (Crampton Ballads, vol. 8, p. 482, British Library 11621 h. 11). Tune: sung by William Bartlett, Wimborne Union, Dorset; collected by H. E. D. Hammond, 1905 (Stephen Sedley, *The Seeds of Love*, 1967, p. 74, and F. Purslow, *The Wanton Seed*, 1968, p. 26).

121 The Stone Cutter's Boy
Sung by William Stokes (b. 1842), Chew Stoke, Somerset; collected by Cecil Sharp, 27. 8. 1906 (MS no. 1074). Broadside, 'The Stone Cutter Bold', printed by W. Ford, York Street, Sheffield (Selbourne Ballads, Birmingham University Library).

122 The Buttercups All Grow
Sung by George Spicer (b. 1906), West Hoathly, Sussex, on the record, *The Brave Ploughboy* (Transatlantic XTRS 1150, 1975); recorded 1974; produced by Karl Dallas.

123 Morgan Rattler, Or, Darby O'Golicker
Text: slip-song without imprint (Madden Collection, 5/1158). Tune: John Clare MS, *A Collection of Songs, Airs and Dances for the Violin*, 1818, p. 18 (Northampton Public Library).

124 The Jolly Tinker
Sung by Billy Bolton (otherwise as no. 75).

125 The Quarry Bank Mashers
Sung by Mr and Mrs Hadley, Quarry Bank, Staffs; collected by Roy Palmer, 29. 6. 1971.

126 The Bush of Australia
Sung by Walter Pardon, Knapton, Norfolk; collected by Roy Palmer, 29. 3. 1978.

ACKNOWLEDGMENTS

I should like to thank for their material all the singers, collectors, writers and librarians listed in the Sources and Notes. The tune of no. 3 appears by permission of Dr Ellen J. Stekert. Nos. 4, 55 and 100 appear by permission of Mrs W. Craig; 14, 15, 23, 29, 38, 52, 84 and 107, the Library of Congress; 22, 25, 33, the School of Scottish Studies, University of Edinburgh; 36, 40, 50, 91, the EFDSS; 51, Mrs E. Western; 57, Peter Kennedy; 115, the Scottish Texts Society; 121, the Agent to the Cecil Sharp Estate. In several cases I have been unable to trace copyright holders, and should be glad of information as to their whereabouts.

I should also like to thank for their advice and assistance D. Roy Saer, Dr Alan Bruford, Dave Kilkerr, Kenneth S. Goldstein, Mrs W. MacQueen, Mrs U. Vaughan Williams, Keith Gregson, Peter Hall, Dr Hugh Shields, Tony Engle of Topic Records, Bill Leader of Leader Records, Mrs Theresa Thom of the English Folk Dance and Song Society, Peter Freshwater and Mrs Iona Opie. I am grateful to Pat Palmer for musical advice and to Katharine Thomson – yet again – for her invaluable transcriptions.

INDEX OF TITLES AND FIRST LINES